THE CHRISTIAN COUNSELING WORKBOOK SERIES

Learning to Use This Powerful Emotion for Good

HOPE & HEALING FOR UNHEALTHY ANGER

WRITTEN BY

GARY J. OLIVER, TH.M., PH.D.

Cover design by Trenton Haddock
Interior design by Anne McLaughlin, Blue Lake Design

ISBN: 978-1-960624-11-6

Published by AACC Publishing, Forest, Virginia

Printed in the United States

Note: Some of the concepts in this workbook have been adapted from previous works by the author, including *When Anger Hits Home* and *A Woman's Forbidden Emotion,* both co-authored by H. Norman Wright, and *Real Men Have Feelings Too.*

Many of the names and details of the stories in this workbook have been changed to protect anonymity.

Publisher's note: This workbook is not intended to be a substitute for professional help. It is designed to provide information, personal insights, and a path forward toward hope and healing. For diagnosis or treatment of any mental health problem, consult your physician, licensed therapist, psychiatrist, or other trained professional. Neither the author nor the AACC shall be liable for any physical, psychological, emotional, financial, or commercial damages, including but not limited to special, incidental, consequential, or other damages. Mental health conditions are complex and best evaluated by a physical examination and consultation with a qualified clinician, with an agreed-upon personalized treatment plan to follow.

Table of Contents

Dear Friend,

Our team developed this *Hope & Healing* workbook series for those who are struggling with nagging emotional pain, a crushing sense of loss, and/or mental health challenges in their everyday lives and want to bring God into the equation as they look forward to a better future. We've chosen these topics because people have told us they need resources to deal with these complex and difficult problems.

This series is also designed for our members—counselors, coaches, chaplains, pastors, and others—to complement and increase their effectiveness in care and counseling ministry.

Featuring some of the world's leading experts, each subject is based on the latest research and best practices, overflows with the love and grace of God, and is anchored in His Word. In short, these workbooks provide roadmaps that are clinically excellent and distinctively Christian.

We pray that God will set your feet on a path to new life, and you will be deeply encouraged by the wisdom, compassion, and care flowing from each page.

We can't wait for you to start, and we look forward to hearing how God works in and through you. Our hope is in Him.

> Now to him who is able to do far more abundantly than all that we ask or think, according to the power at work within us, to him be glory in the church and in Christ Jesus throughout all generations, forever and ever. Amen. (Ephesians 3:20-21 ESV)

God be with you. We love being a part of your life.

Sincerely,

Dr. Tim Clinton
President
American Association of Christian Counselors

INTRODUCTION

"Anger is the most powerful emotion."

Many people draw this conclusion because they've seen the impact of explosive rage or bitter resentment "up close and personal." But anger is much more complex than that. Indeed, some people express their anger in explosive ways, but others are more subtle, using passive-aggressive behavior to punish and control others. And many feel so uncomfortable with anger that they shove it down and insist, "I'm fine. Nothing is bothering me."

Anger may be the most prominent and powerful emotion, but it's really a secondary emotion, the result of primary emotions and perceptions that may not be acknowledged at all—feelings of unrelieved hurt, nagging frustrations, and a multitude of fears. If these deeper issues aren't identified and addressed, the surface emotion and expression of anger rarely change.

But anger isn't necessarily a villain; it can actually be a gift. Yes, a gift. It can be a healthy response to perceived injustice, and when directed wisely, it's a powerful force for good. But we're getting ahead of ourselves. Let's look into the lives of a few people whose anger controls them.

Snapshots

"Recently, I've realized that I'm afraid of my feelings," Carl said softly as we talked in my counseling office. After a long pause, he added, "I don't know who I am emotionally, and it scares me to death. I don't think I even know how or what to feel."

Carl had been the successful pastor of a large evangelical church for seven years. He prided himself on how hard he worked and how much of his time was spent "serving the Lord." His devotion (addiction) to work had been viewed as "godly dedication," and he pressured his staff to work as hard as he did. If you had talked with him two years earlier, he would have told you that he had the perfect marriage, family, and ministry.

But when Carl's oldest child became a freshman in high school, he "fell in with the wrong crowd." At about the same time, his wife became more assertive about her frustration with their lack of meaningful communication and intimacy. Two people on his board asked to meet with him: the first one said Carl was pushing his team too hard and needed to be more affirming, and the other complained that Carl wasn't doing enough in several areas of the church's ministry.

Carl felt hurt, angry, and afraid that his carefully choreographed life was unraveling. It was. Suddenly, the easy answers weren't working anymore. He began to lose his enthusiasm for ministry. He became frustrated at little things that never would have bothered him before. He became increasingly critical—of his kids, his wife, his team, and anyone who dared to be the least bit resistant to him—but when people noticed and asked what was bothering him, he insisted, "Nothing. I'm fine." Carl had no idea how to cope with his powerful emotions.

Jessica is a successful business manager for a large company. For years, she was respected for her "commitment" and "dependability." Around the office, she was known as the one who could always be counted on to get the job done . . . no matter what was required of her. The office motto was, "If you need something done, ask Jessica." At church, she was respected for her "unselfishness" and her "servant's heart." Her friends at church also knew her to be the kind of person who wouldn't say no to any request.

However, during the past six months, something in Jessica had changed. Her eagerness to help had morphed into bitterness. She found herself withdrawing from activities she had enjoyed, and she started avoiding people. More recently, her anger had a hair trigger—she had to fight her compulsion to tell people off. Her best friend tried to talk to her several times to find out what was happening with her, but Jessica now saw herself as a victim and felt completely justified with her resentment. One night, as she relived conversations throughout the day to find fault with people, she realized how far she'd slipped from the positive, dependable person she'd been. She wondered, *What happened to me?*

Marlene grew up in a small midwestern community where her parents were leaders in the local church. In her home, any mention of emotions was strictly off-limits. She'd never heard her parents say, "I love you," and doesn't remember seeing them demonstrate any love toward each other. The only display of emotions she could remember was hearing her parents yelling at each other behind closed doors. This was usually followed by several days of her parents not talking to each other. She recalled, "It wasn't okay to express feelings in my family. At an early age, we built emotional dams to keep from feeling any pain. I think it was a way to avoid falling into our fear and our sadness . . . and not being able to climb out again."

Phil had a very different problem with anger. When he started dating Melinda, he'd kept most of his anger in check, but she increasingly got on his nerves after they married. The "little things" that once had seemed so cute now infuriated him. A month after their wedding, he exploded at Melinda: "Can't you do anything right!" She had sensed something was really bothering him, but she had no idea it was her! For the next ten years, Phil used his anger—and more often, the threat of his anger—to intimidate Melinda into submission. On several occasions, she thought he was going to hit her. He would grab her, but he always stopped short of punching her or throwing her to the ground . . . yet she suspected that day was coming.

Melinda is the one who came to see me. When I asked if Phil would join her for the next session, she cried, "I hope he will. I hope he will." The following week, Phil came in, sat down, crossed his arms, and barely said a word. When they left, I was sure Melinda would pay a steep price for asking me for help.

Carl, Jessica, Marlene, and Melinda all asked me for help dealing with anger. They'd realized that how they reacted to anger was a problem, but they weren't yet aware of the root problem: none of them understood the *source* of this powerful emotion and how to deal with it.

Somewhere along the line, Carl, Jessica, and Marlene had decided their feelings couldn't be trusted, weren't important, and didn't count . . . or were too uncomfortable and threatening. So, they'd stopped listening to their feelings, ignored them, and tried to make them disappear. They pursued excellence and kept a busy schedule to keep them from reflecting and feeling. They invested countless hours in helping people (which isn't bad), but they were so busy helping others that they didn't care for their own hearts (which isn't good). Their busyness was an effective yet short-term anesthetic for their painful emotions. Phil used a different strategy: he wielded his powerful anger as a tool to intimidate and control Melinda.

The stories of Carl, Jessica, Marlene, and Phil and Melinda are like those of literally thousands of people who have come to me for counseling. Their frustration and pain are all too common. For a variety of reasons, they concluded their painful emotions—chiefly hurt, fear, anger, and shame—made them feel too vulnerable, so they put them in a bottle and screwed the top on tight. Some can keep their emotions bottled up for years, but others, like Phil, have learned that anger gives them power.

Our emotions, and in fact, the full range of emotions, are part of what it means to be created "in the image of God." In the Gospels, we see Jesus express joy, love, compassion, and gratitude, but also sorrow and anger. As we experience more of God's magnificent grace, we can grow and gradually become a little more like Jesus. This means that *having* the full range of emotions is like him, but our challenge is to learn how to *express* those emotions in healthy ways like he did. So, it's not wrong to feel painful and powerful emotions like anger, but we need to learn how to understand the cause and then express our anger in ways that honor God and respect people.

I can relate to Carl, Jessica, and Marlene because I have a similar story. I was raised in a conservative, fundamental, Bible-believing church. I went to Sunday School for twelve years without missing a Sunday. I had memorized hundreds of Bible verses. But I was never taught the source or role or importance of emotions in the Christian life. It's taken years to learn the lessons I'm communicating in this workbook. So, as you work to understand what's behind your anger and wrestle with getting your emotions under control, remember . . . I'm one of you.

When you were growing up, how did your parents model (positively or negatively) the full range of emotions, from joy and love to anger and grief?

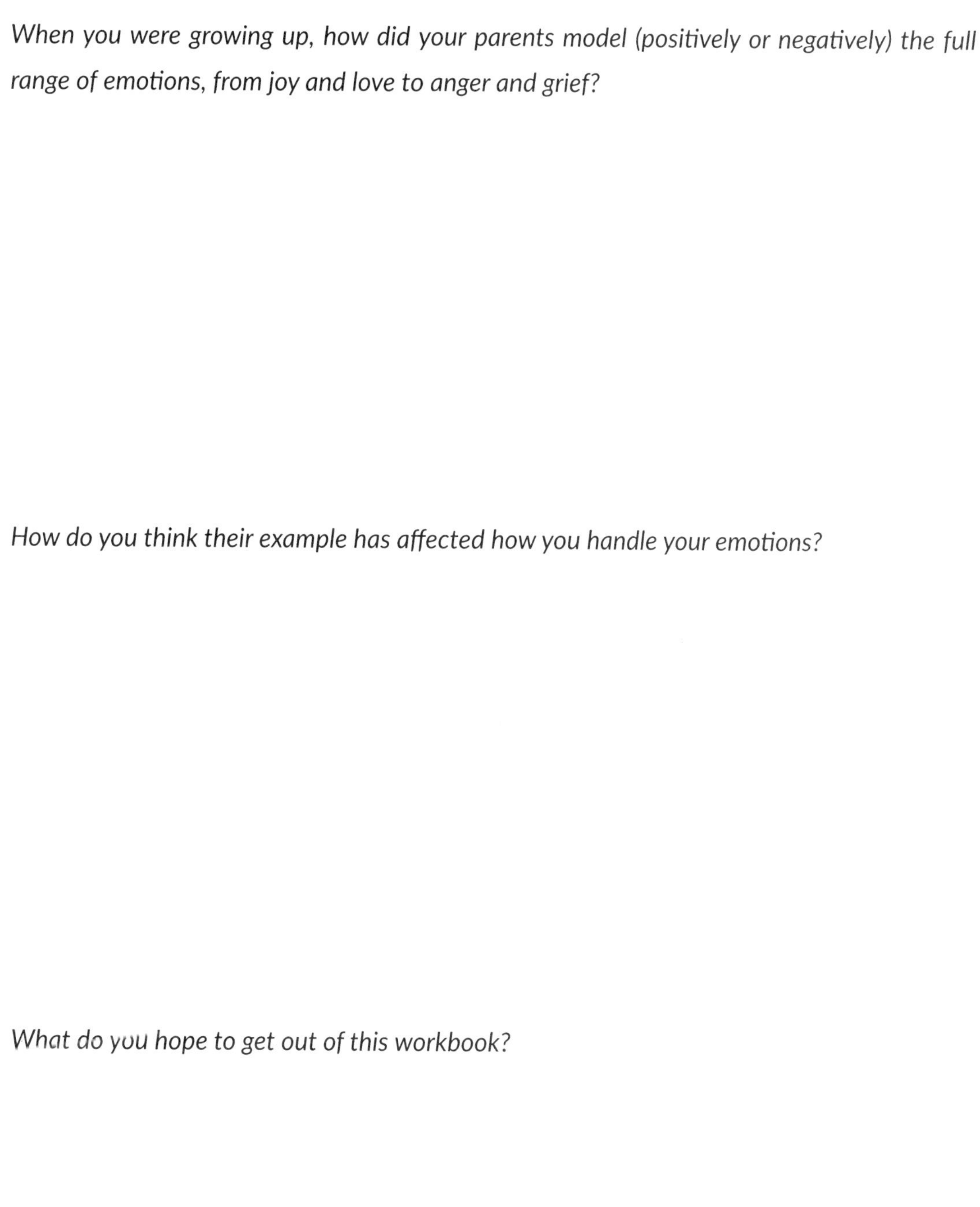

How do you think their example has affected how you handle your emotions?

What do you hope to get out of this workbook?

CHAPTER 1

MADE IN GOD'S IMAGE

Before we move into the specifics of anger, we first need a basic understanding of emotions—all of them. Until we understand what emotions are, where they come from, why God gave them to us, and how they function, we'll have only limited success in dealing with specific emotions, especially anger. We need to realize that emotions are standard equipment for everyone.

In my work, I've realized that many Christians have an especially difficult time living with their emotions. Christ died and rose again to make a difference in our lives. Unfortunately, though, for many believers the difference is primarily external or, at best, intellectual. They don't know what to do with their emotions, so they live like a dormant volcano: they hope the plug holding the magma chamber holds so their emotions don't explode and spew out over everything! But it's inevitable—explosions happen, and then they feel intense shame for being out of control. No matter how hard they try to ignore or repress their feelings, their lives are still dominated by hurt, frustration, and fear, which are the three primary sources of anger. They've become stuck in relational and emotional ruts and rarely experience the joy of their salvation.

Many believers get discouraged and feel guilty because they still have those struggles. This creates a problem. We instinctively ask ourselves, *Should I share my questions and struggles with others and risk appearing immature and unspiritual? Or do I stuff, repress, suppress, deny, or ignore my emotions and pretend that everything's going great?*

Rather than risk the humiliation and possible rejection that might come from sharing their feelings, many Christians try to ignore their problems and stuff their emotions. Eventually, however, this creates an even more significant issue. We can only fake it for so long.

Do you know anyone who tries really hard to keep the plug in the magma chamber of their emotions in place? What are some consequences?

Made New?

For many Christians, part of the problem originates from a misunderstanding of 2 Corinthians 5:17. In the King James translation, we read: "Therefore if any man be in Christ, he is a new creature: old things are passed away; behold, all things are become new." I've heard some preachers state that if you still struggle with old patterns of feeling, thinking, and behaving, then it's clear that *all* things haven't become new . . . and maybe you aren't really saved!

This view misunderstands the context of the passage. In 2 Corinthians, Paul is describing our destiny of being with God forever. When he says "all things are new," he means "all things related to eternal life." When we trust Jesus, that changes immediately, radically, and forever! What doesn't change is our bodies, our personalities, our memories, and many other aspects of who we are. We still live in a fallen world. We have been gloriously saved from the *penalty* of sin; as we walk with Christ, the *power* of sin is gradually eroded in us, and someday, we'll be with Jesus in the new heavens and new earth, and we'll never experience the *presence* of sin again!

Yet for now we live between *the already* and *the not yet*. We've already been saved, we have the- Holy Spirit living inside us, and we have God's "precious and magnificent promises," but the total fulfillment of those promises won't happen until we see Jesus face to face. So even though I trusted Jesus to save me, my *mind* didn't become more intelligent, nor did my old, painful memories disappear overnight. As for my *emotions,* I found I still struggled with anger, lust, and depression. In the area of the *will,* my deeply ingrained habit patterns didn't magically vanish. The process of "becoming conformed to the image of [God's] Son" (Romans 8:29) takes time. Maturity is indeed a process. It's clear that part of the process of spiritual growth involves the healing of our damaged emotions.

How might it be helpful to realize we live in tension between what God has already done for us and in us in Christ . . . and what God promises to fulfill when we see Jesus face to face?

In His Image

In the opening chapters of the Bible, we learn that Adam and Eve were created in God's image, meaning that God created humans with a mind, emotions, and a will. As his image-bearers, we have the capacity to think, feel, and make choices. Years ago, philosopher and theologian Francis Schaeffer wrote, "As God is a person, He feels, thinks, and acts: so I am a person, who feels, thinks and acts."[1] Even though the image of God in men and women was damaged and distorted by sin, we are still image-bearers.

Emotions are important. We have emotions because God has emotions, and we're made in his image. Emotions are intended by God, designed by God, and created by God to enrich our lives and to be a powerful and positive force for good. Emotions enhance our ability to be in a relationship with him and one another. However, due to the Fall and the effects of sin, our emotions, like our minds and our wills, have become damaged and distorted. For many, the emotions God intended to make our lives more meaningful instead make life more miserable.

Many people are surprised to discover how much the Bible says about emotions. From Genesis through Revelation, we read about God's emotions and those of the people he created. In the New Testament, we find that Christ experienced and expressed a wide range of emotions, including love, compassion, joy, fear, sorrow, disappointment, discouragement, frustration, hurt, rejection, loneliness, and anger.

Our emotions influence almost every aspect of our lives. God speaks to us through our emotions. They're like a sixth sense. Emotions help us monitor our needs, make us aware of good and evil, and provide motivation and energy for growth and change. Emotions give us the vigor, force, and power for living. Emotions are energy in motion.

Is it difficult to believe that part of being made in the image of God is experiencing the full range of emotions? Explain your answer.

Three Reactions to Emotions

Sin has led to two unhealthy reactions to emotions. The first is to deny or ignore them. The reason we're reluctant to acknowledge our emotions is that we're terrified of them! They're too powerful, too threatening, and they make us feel out of control . . . and vulnerable. Unfortunately, ignoring or minimizing life's emotional realities distorts our perspective, limits our perception, and leads us to distrust our experience. We often deny or ignore the very things God intends to use to help us grow.

The second unhealthy reaction is to allow our emotions to control us. This is an equally dangerous position. Powerful emotions can be overwhelming, dominating our thoughts and directing our actions. For instance, after God led the Israelites out of slavery in Egypt and right to the edge of the Promised Land, it was *fear* that limited their ability to recall what God had done for them—and necessitated another forty years in the wilderness until a more faithful generation was able to enter (Numbers 13—14). When Saul heard of David's popularity and success after his defeat of Goliath, it was overwhelming *jealousy* that interfered with Saul's ability to learn from his mistakes (1 Samuel 18—20). And even after Elijah's powerful demonstration of God's power in his confrontation with the priests of Baal on Mount Carmel, the prophet was immediately beset by various consuming emotions, causing him to lose perspective and want to die (1 Kings 18—19).

Resisting emotions, or letting emotions control us: does either reaction offer much hope?

What happens when we make the mistake of ignoring or stuffing our emotions? What's the expected payoff? What are some of the usual consequences?

What happens when we make the mistake of expressing our emotions in unhealthy ways? What payoff are we looking for? What are some of the real consequences?

By God's grace, we have a *third option* for how to respond to our emotions. We can choose to view them from God's perspective and bring them into harmony with our minds. Maturity involves the whole person. *It's impossible to be spiritually mature and emotionally immature.* True maturity requires a balance between our head, our heart, and our will—a combination of thinking, feeling, and doing. Each aspect is important. God designed each one for our good. Each one is a manifestation of the image of God in us.

An essential part of sanctification (or spiritual growth) is healing our damaged emotions. God wants to help us recover from the effects of sin in this vital dimension of our personality, to restore the healthy balance God designed between our ability to think, feel, and choose.

Do you agree or disagree that it's impossible to be spiritually mature and emotionally immature? Explain your answer.

What Are Emotions?

When I'm speaking to groups and ask them to define emotions, their most common response is, "Emotions are what I feel." That's a true statement, and many people use "feelings" and "emotions" interchangeably, yet that's not a definition. It's somewhat like trying to define air by saying, "Air is what I breathe." Most people are surprised that something as familiar as emotions can be so difficult to define.

King David once asserted, "I am fearfully and wonderfully made" (Psalm 139:14). In no place is the complexity of God's creation more evident than in our emotional makeup. Our experience of emotions involves sensory, skeletal, motor, autonomic, and cognitive aspects.

We can define *emotion* in several different ways. Webster's official definition is "a psychic and physical reaction subjectively experienced as strong feeling and physiologically involving changes that prepare the body for immediate vigorous action." The word *emotion* is derived from the Latin word *emovare* which means "to move" or "having to do with motion, movement, and energy." I heard a speaker suggest that *emotion* should be spelled "E-motion" since emotions are "energy in motion."

What are some of the most common emotions? In seminars and worships, I've asked participants to list their frequently experienced emotions. Various groups have come up with lists ranging from as few as 11 to as many as 82 expressions of what they classified as emotions. (Would you be surprised to learn that the group that came up with only 11 was a men's group, and the list of 82 came from a women's group? I didn't think so.) Some of the most commonly identified emotions have included:

loved	happy	pleased	surprised
confused	confident	anxious	concerned
indifferent	fearful	hurt	frustrated
embarrassed	frightened	humiliated	angry
appreciated	accepted	excited	grieving
scared	lonely	proud	terrified
bored	glad	elated	worried
delighted	uncomfortable	shamed	generous
depressed	unsure	sad	

Sometimes, the experience of a shocking event makes us more aware of our emotions. Tom was a tall and athletic man in his mid-fifties. He had grown up on the Sand Hills of western Nebraska and had been a cattle rancher all his life. When he came into my office, the first thing he said was, "I want you to know that I'm just not an emotional kind of guy." He went on to explain that some people, especially women, have a lot of emotions, and some people don't. He was convinced that he was someone who didn't have (or need) many emotions. His philosophy had worked for most of his life, but recently, land values had dropped and he found out his wife had cancer. Consequently, his perceived emotion-free world had begun to crumble.

Some people are more aware of their emotions than others, but the experience of emotions isn't optional. Regardless of gender, age, race, or socioeconomic level, emotions are standard equipment. The only option we have is how we *choose* to express them. I can't always choose *what* I feel, but I can choose how long I feel it and *how I respond to it*. With God's help, we can change our emotional patterns.

Emotional maturity requires an awareness of specific characteristics of emotions. One of the most helpful ways to understand emotions is to examine some traits they share. Let's look at seven essential principles that help us understand our emotional lives.

1. God created all emotions. There aren't any good or bad, healthy or unhealthy emotions.

I've read several authors and heard different speakers who have talked about emotions as good and bad, right and wrong, constructive and destructive. I even heard someone give one list of emotions we should cultivate and another list we should avoid at all costs.

Of all the emotions, anger is most often viewed as a "negative" emotion. When anger is out of control, it can have a devastating effect, but anger itself isn't healthy or unhealthy. In fact, the majority of references to anger in the Bible are about God's anger. Anger, like all the others, is a God-given emotion. It can provide a source of power that can be used for good or evil. It's the impact, not the feeling itself, that can be constructive or destructive. In this workbook, you'll see that when we understand our anger and choose to express it in healthy ways, it has enormous potential for good.

We can have healthy or unhealthy reactions to all our emotions. The extent to which we understand what emotions are, where they come from, and their role in our lives will, to a great degree, determine their effect on us and others. For example, most people view love as a positive emotion, but when we allow love to get out of control or we attach love to the wrong person or thing, it can close our eyes to reality and have a devastating effect. For example, narcissism involves an immature, self-centered, and inordinate love of self that narrows our world and limits our ability to grow. It was a narcissist who wrote:

> I love myself, I think I'm grand
> I go to the movies and I hold my hand,
> I put my arms around my waist,
> And when I get fresh I slap my face.[2]

People speak of good vs. bad emotions because they fail to distinguish an emotion from the behaviors that express it. Maturity involves distinguishing between the emotion—the mental arousal and the corresponding physiological changes—and how we choose to express that emotion. What a person *feels* is one thing. What one *chooses to do* in either expressing or reacting to that emotion is another.

The expression of an emotion can be constructive or destructive. The degree to which our emotions help us or hinder us depends on how well we acknowledge them, understand them, choose to channel them through our thought life, and view them from a balanced, healthy perspective.

Before reading this section, would you have said some emotions are "bad" or "negative"? If so, how has that perspective shaped your view of your emotions?

2. It's possible to have strong emotions and not be aware of them.

One of the psychological tests I use in my counseling and consulting practice measures hostility. On one occasion, a couple came to see me. It didn't take long for me to see the need to use this test with the husband—he scored 96 out of a possible 100 points! When I started to discuss this with him, he interrupted and shouted, "These test results are wrong! I AM NOT an angry man!" The expression on his wife's face told me the real story. It was difficult for this intelligent and well-educated Christian to admit that he was sometimes controlled by his unhealthy anger.

How do you think the man's wife felt at that moment?

Why do you imagine he felt so threatened?

3. Emotions have physical effects.

When we experience our emotions, changes in our central nervous system involve chemicals and neurotransmitters, and our peripheral nervous system is affected. When feeling certain emotions, you might experience a more rapid heartbeat, dilated pupils, increased perspiration, trembling, tears, goosebumps, a tremendous surge of energy, or a sense of exhaustion/fatigue.

Such physical effects can be serious . . . sometimes deadly serious. A study by the National Institutes of Health looked at the connection between chronic anger and heart disease. Psychologist Laurie Friedman Donze, program officer for the organization that funded the study, explains, "We've long suspected, based on observational studies, that anger can negatively affect the heart. This study in healthy adults helps fill a real knowledge gap and shows how this might occur. It also opens the door to promoting anger management interventions as a way to potentially help stave off heart disease, the leading cause of death in this country." Similarly, Daichi Shimbo, a cardiologist at the Columbia University Medical Center, warns, "If you're a person who gets angry all the time, you're having chronic injuries to your blood vessels. It's these chronic injuries over time that may eventually cause irreversible effects on vascular health and eventually increase your heart disease risk."[3] To live longer and be healthy, we need to control the intensity and frequency of our anger.

4. Emotions have a stimulus-response effect.

We usually experience emotions in response to a thought that occurs in our inner world or an event that occurs in our outer world. This is an example of how thinking and feeling are related. When we have a new experience, we attach emotions to it depending upon our reactive (often unacknowledged) interpretation of what happened. Those reactions can become a habit, and those habits become a part of our reflexive emotional patterns. For many of us, our emotional patterns are unconscious and automatic.

Let's look at a simple example: Whenever I hear the hymn "When I Survey The Wondrous Cross," I'm incredibly moved. I often get tears in my eyes and a lump in my throat, and I sometimes have a difficult time singing. I don't remember when I first heard this classic hymn. It was uneventful, and the song had no more meaning than most others, but as I've gotten older, the words in the song have taken on a whole new meaning. Now, I can even hear an instrumental version of it on the radio and experience an emotionally moving response.

5. Most emotional reactions are learned.

Interestingly, people can have different emotional responses to the same event. The kind of emotion we experience is, to a great degree, determined by the meaning or interpretation we often unconsciously make of that event. What excites and energizes one person can bring panic and emotional paralysis to another. Several factors influence our emotional responses, including childhood experiences, where we were raised, our denominational background, and our personality type.

One of the most important factors is our home environment. Some of us grew up in homes where healthy emotions weren't modeled, and it was off-limits even to mention them. The few emotions that were expressed were often explosive, reactive, shaming, and blaming . . . and then stuffed. There were no labels for the emotions and no healthy opportunities to understand them, let alone know what to do with them.

Others grew up in homes where emotions weren't merely ignored. Emotional expression was punished, and emotional repression was reinforced. Children raised in this environment either consciously or unconsciously tell themselves that it isn't safe to feel. For survival, their minds were trained to stuff, repress, suppress, deny, or ignore emotions, filter them out, and if one accidentally crept up to the surface, stuff it back down.

In this kind of environment, they weren't taught to identify and understand emotions, and they weren't free to experience their God-given emotions in healthy ways. The only thing that felt safe was not to feel, so they became emotionally numb. Now, as adults, they're faced with the difficult task of unlearning old dysfunctional patterns and replacing them with healthy new patterns—which is easier said than done.

Another significant factor is gender. Many men grew up in homes where being a "man's man" was equated with being unemotional. Society didn't reward or honor sensitive men, so we saw very few models of male emotional authenticity. If a man displayed any emotion, it was most likely anger, and it was probably an unhealthy expression. Many men didn't even know how to spell intimacy, let alone what it meant. Many of us grew up as emotional illiterates, so when we come face-to-face with situations that force us to deal with emotions, we don't have any idea what to do. On the other hand, women were allowed to express a wide range of emotions, yet many weren't taught how to make sense of them or communicate them in healthy ways.

How did the modeling of your parents and the environment in your childhood home affect how you view emotions?

6. If we don't understand and control our emotions, they'll control us.

Several years ago, I had the opportunity to speak to mothers of preschoolers who had asked me to talk about emotions. When I stated that it's essential to understand and control our emotions, one woman took offense and raised her hand to disagree. She had interpreted my use of the term "control" to mean keeping emotions in check by ignoring or stuffing them. I thanked her for allowing me to clarify an important point.

Ignoring emotions isn't an option for anyone who wants to be healthy and mature. Paradoxically, it takes an enormous amount of energy to ignore your emotions! And even then, we can't ignore them indefinitely. We can only anesthetize ourselves just so long. Emotional repression may eventually lead to self-destructive and relationally destructive behaviors and addictions such as working too much, eating too little, eating too much, alcohol and drug dependence, compulsive spending, sexual addictions, not sleeping enough, sleeping too much, controlling behaviors, obsessive thinking, and other compulsive patterns.

My use of *control* meant to guide or manage, much like the skill needed to properly use a tool. A professional craftsman has a variety of tools in a tool chest. Learning how to use those tools effectively and safely takes time and effort. The effectiveness of the tool depends on the craftsman's skill. Some tools are effective in certain situations but totally ineffective in others.

Our emotions are like tools. As an "emotional craftsman," learning about our emotions takes time and effort. Through trial and error, we learn when we can trust our emotions and when we can't. When I talk about controlling our emotions, I'm talking about increasing our skills in understanding them and managing how we choose to express them. Healthy people get regular practice in being aware of their emotions. They're more likely to understand themselves and better equipped to perceive the feelings of others.

What are some ways, if any, that strong emotions have controlled your responses to threats and opportunities?

7. Shared emotions are the currency of healthy relationships.

Unfortunately, many of us don't know how to share our emotions. The more intense and painful the emotion, the more difficult it is to share. Even those with years of training in communicating their *ideas* with clarity may have precious little training in understanding, let alone clearly communicating their *feelings*. When they try, they come on too strong or not strong enough. They may cry, laugh, or get angry at the "wrong" time. It's embarrassing, and others misunderstand, so they decide it's safer to avoid the risk of the humiliation of being rejected or laughed at, so they stop sharing.

Emotions help us understand ourselves and others. If we conceal our emotions, they become more difficult to understand, but when we express our emotions, we can confirm or correct what we're feeling. Withholding our emotions can distort our view of the world and isolate us from others. When we don't share our emotions, others don't know what's most important to us.

Emotions are made to be expressed. They are the currency of healthy relationships. They provide the passion and intensity needed to initiate and sustain meaningful relationships. John Powell said, "I can only know that much of myself which I have had the courage to confide to you."[4] Expressing our emotions helps us and others better understand *who* we are and *what's* important to us.

Who is someone who makes you feel safe? How much have you been honest and vulnerable with that person?

Small Beginnings

Let me offer some practical steps you can take to be more in touch with your emotions.

1. Thank God for making you in his image. Thank him for your mind, emotions, and will—and for the ability to think, feel, and choose.
2. Ask God to help you understand the role of emotions in becoming a mature and healthy man or woman. Don't be afraid of your emotions. See them for what they are—a gift from God. Be open to learning about your emotions, especially anger.
3. Examine what the Bible says about emotions. Read about David and note the role of emotions in his life. As you read through the Gospels, examine the life of Christ. What kinds of emotions did he experience, and how did he choose to express them?
4. Observe your emotional pattern. Look back at the list of common emotions in this chapter.
    - *What emotions do you frequently experience?*
    - *Which ones do you rarely experience?*
    - *What emotions are easy for you to express?*

› *Which ones are difficult for you to express?*

› *What aspect of your emotional pattern would you like to change?*

5. Pick one emotion you want to understand better, believing God would have you develop more effective skills in expressing it.

   › *Identify the emotion.*

   › *Define it.*

   › *Make a list of what you consider unhealthy and healthy expressions of it.*

- *Can you identify any models from Scripture showing healthy expressions of that emotion?*

What are three specific ways you might begin to change your unhealthy reactive pattern into a healthy response pattern?

CHAPTER 2

THE GIFT OF HEALTHY ANGER

What comes to mind when you hear the word *love* . . . or *kindness* . . . or *compassion*? You may think of someone who has treated you in ways that reflect these words. You may remember times when you experienced supportive, loving connections with people, but now grieve those days long gone. Or you may get a sinking feeling in your gut because affection and attention seem like pipedreams. Whatever our backgrounds, these words surface either gratitude or desire . . . and maybe both.

But what comes to mind when you hear the word *anger*? Flashbacks of your mother or father yelling at you? An instant recollection of when someone hurt you? Memories of endless nights seething with resentment for what people have done to you? Or do you see fury as an ally, helping you control people?

Over the years, I've conducted many retreats to help people understand the full range of God-given emotions, and I can confidently affirm that when they walked through the door on the first night, almost every single person viewed anger as "a negative and even dangerous emotion." It's crucial to understand that the *feeling* of anger isn't wrong or negative, but our actions in response to it can be either constructive or destructive. The problem, of course, is that most of the time, the reactions we observe—in ourselves and others—are destructive, so we tend to believe that all anger is wrong and sinful. As we'll see, that's simply not true.

What comes to mind (memories, word associations, and feelings) when you hear the word "love"?

What comes to mind when you hear the word "anger"?

Definitions

Most of us are aware that unhealthy anger is (or certainly can be) a huge problem. At a men's conference years ago, three breakout sessions were offered: (1) Relating to your spouse and children; (2) Handling finances; and (3) Dealing with anger. Of the 300 men who attended, 250 came to the one on anger!

Anger is notoriously difficult to define. The Merriam-Webster dictionary defines it as "a strong feeling of displeasure and usually of opposition toward someone or something." Others say anger is "a response to a perceived threat." At its best, it's a response to injustice. When anger rises in us, we can ask ourselves, *What am I protecting or defending?* The list of possibilities is endless, including our comfort, our reputations, our safety and security, our political views, our families, etc., etc., etc.

God's anger is often in response to injustice inflicted on those he loves. When we experience anger because those God loves suffer injustice, our response is in line with his—especially when our anger empowers us to speak the truth in love, defend the weak, and care for the brokenhearted. But God's anger is always measured, never an out-of-control reaction. In several places in the Scriptures, the writers tell us that God is "slow to anger, abounding in love and faithfulness" (Psalm 86:15, et al.).

Before reading this section, what was your definition (or description) of anger?

What are some reasons it's important to grasp that at its best, anger is a good and godly response to injustice?

How We Experience Anger

What follows may seem like a strange and unnecessary section of the chapter, but believe me, it's important! In my conversations with people over the years, I've seen several distinct ways people feel and express their anger, including:

- ***Gas and a match***

  This is perhaps how most of us think of angry people. It doesn't take much for something (anything!) to trigger an outburst of rage. Some people get over it quickly, but for others, quick rage turns into lasting suspicion and resentment.

- ***Mount St. Helens***

  Have you seen the footage of the day this long-dormant volcano in the Northwest exploded? Some people are like that. It might take them a long time to "blow their top," but when they do, watch out! The blast radius can be wide, and the devastation severe.

- ***Slow burn***

  I've known some people who aren't demonstrative with their anger . . . at least, not right away. This is the "I don't get mad; I get even" group. They don't blow up, they don't lose control, and they don't use anger to intimidate. Instead, they go into stealth mode, looking for the right time to get revenge—"a dish," they like to say, "that is best served cold."

› *Conflicted*

When sensitive and reflective people get angry, they tend to spout off, and then feel terribly guilty for being "mean" and "out of control." Their fury is coupled with shame because they couldn't control themselves, they've played a fool in public, and they don't know how to fix it.

› *Anesthetized*

And then there are those who feel so unsafe, so insecure, so afraid of what would happen if they expressed anger (or anything remotely resembling anger) that they shove those emotions down into the deepest recesses of their souls. For some reason, years before, they intuitively concluded that being numb was safer than understanding and being in touch with their powerful feelings.

Have any names and faces come to mind as you've considered the various ways people feel their anger?

And how about you? Which category best represents how you feel anger? Or do you feel it in different ways, based on the person and the situation?

The Faces of Anger

People may feel anger in a similar way but express it very differently. Some of the faces of anger parallel the way people feel the emotion, but not always. Take a look . . .

› *The Bully*

Most of us are familiar with someone in this category. Bullies use anger to manipulate through intimidation. Oh, they can be charming and polite when they don't feel threatened, but when they're challenged, they "get big"—rising up in their chair, increasing the volume, glaring, and commanding the room.

› *The Sniper*

In the Special Forces, a sniper finds a secluded place, sets up his high-powered rifle on a tripod, assesses the distance, wind, and elevation, and takes a lethal shot. I've seen people sit in a room looking cool and collected, but all the while, they were marking their target, planning their best shot, and waiting for an ideal moment when the victim was unaware of the coming blast of anger. Snipers use sharp criticism to cut people to shreds, and they always have a comeback when anyone challenges them.

› *Just Kidding!*

Some people are masters at disguise. They use harsh sarcasm to put people down, and if anyone objects, they claim, "Hey, I was only joking!" They refuse to admit their words were meant to harm, and in fact, they're often supported by onlookers who laugh at their inappropriate "humor." These people also may use passive-aggressive techniques, like habitually being late if the other person likes to be on time, just to get under the person's skin.

› *Truth with grace*

Is it possible to be a wise, strong, secure person who expresses anger at injustice in the right way at the right time? Yes, that's what this workbook is about! Jesus was (and is) our model of loving people enough to tell them the truth and do it in a kind and loving way. He tailored his words to fit the person and the circumstance. His tenderness and clear directive to the woman caught in adultery (John 8:1-11) were coupled with protecting her from the angry, self-righteous religious leaders. His fierce rebuttal of those leaders was necessary because they were hurting people for the sake of their own power and prestige. We want to get to the point in our growth that our anger becomes fuel for good, propelling us to protect the vulnerable, lovingly correct the wayward, and hold people accountable when they're harming others.

Think about when you were growing up and match each family member with one of the faces of anger.

Which one is the face you see when you look in the mirror?

Ten Truths

Believe it or not (and I hope you'll believe it by the end of this chapter!), your anger can be a positive force for good. For that to happen, we need to have a deeper understanding of its dynamics.

1. Anger is a God-given emotion.

As we've seen, we're created in God's image. For him, anger is a right and good response to harm inflicted on people, as well as a right and good response to those who reject him. In the span of just a few verses in Paul's letter to the Ephesians, the apostle gives seemingly contradictory instructions. He writes, "Be angry and do not sin"—a positive command to be angry followed by a warning: "do not let the sun go down on your anger" (4:26). But five verses later, he commanded, "Let all bitterness and wrath and anger and clamor and slander be put away from you, along with all malice. Be kind to one another, tenderhearted, forgiving one another, as God in Christ forgave you" (vss. 31-32).

There are times, then, when the only appropriate response to a person or a situation is godly anger, a kind of anger that is expressed very differently from the ungodly, destructive kind. Godly anger prompts us to put love into action to defend the vulnerable; the other kind compels us to despise people who are created in the image of God.

It may be surprising to realize that it's just as wrong to disobey the command to "be angry" as it is to ignore the instruction to "put away" bitterness, wrath, anger, slander, and malice. Centuries ago, church leader John Chrysostom wrote, "He who is not angry, whereas he has cause to be, sins. For unreasonable patience is the hotbed of many vices, it fosters negligence, and incites not only the wicked but the good to do wrong." Let me paraphrase: If there's a good reason to be angry and you don't get angry, it makes you emotionally numb and passive, allowing abusers to continue to abuse!

How would you paraphrase Chrysostom's quote or explain it to a friend?

2. Anger is a secondary emotion.

Anger is usually the first emotion we see in ourselves and others, but it's often a cover for some other emotion(s). Anger can be prompted by hurt, frustration, fear, and/or shame hidden beneath the visible display. Many of us have learned either that anger is a powerful way to intimidate others, so we justify it, or it makes us feel out of control, so we stuff it. We (especially men) feel more comfortable with anger than the deeper, more threatening emotions. But we'd be wise to "look under the hood" to identify the engine driving our anger.

What are some reasons people don't want to "look under the hood" to identify primary emotions?

3. Anger is a signal.

Anger is like the shriek of the smoke detector when the house is on fire, or the flashing light on the dashboard telling us there's a problem with the car. If we pay attention, we can respond appropriately; if we don't, we'll react in immature and unhealthy ways, and suffer the consequences. In her book, *The Dance of Anger*, Harriett Lerner observes,

> Anger is a signal, and one worth listening to. Our anger may be a message that we are being hurt, that our rights are being violated, that our needs or wants are not being adequately met, or simply that something is not right. Our anger may tell us that we are not addressing an important emotional issue in our lives, or that too much of our self—our beliefs, values, desires, or ambitions—is being compromised in a relationship. Our anger may be a signal that we are doing more and giving more than we can comfortably do or give. Or, our anger may warn us that others are doing too much for us, at the expense of our own competence and growth.

> Just as physical pain tells us to take our hand off the hot stove, the pain of our anger preserves the very integrity of our self. Our anger can motivate us to say "no" to the ways in which we are defined by others and "yes" to the dictates of our inner self.[5]

Do you take action when the smoke detector goes off at your house? Of course, you do. It's what any sane person does.

What difference does it make to realize anger can be a helpful signal?

4. Managed anger enhances relationships.

Unmanaged anger crushes and confuses the people around us, but a healthy response to anger opens the door to richer, deeper conversations. Couples, families, and friendships grow stronger when we can disagree without having to win or escape. Healthy responses to anger—ours and in the people we care about—strip away false harmony and encourage openness and vulnerability. Trust is built, not shattered or eroded. The *feeling* of anger doesn't strengthen or weaken relationships; it's our *expression* of the feeling that can build or destroy.

This may be a stretch for you, but stay with me. What are some ways addressing your anger can help you build stronger relationships?

5. Anger can help us set limits and boundaries.

One of the most common problems in relationships is the absence (or weakness) of limits and boundaries. Limits say, "This is as far as I'm willing to go"; boundaries say, "This is as far as I'm willing for you to go." Since anger is a response to a threat, real or perceived, it gives us the opportunity to evaluate what's going on. We may realize the emotion has arisen because someone demands more from us than we are able or willing to give, or it may be the result of a person treating us with disrespect. Our anger, then, gives us insight to say yes when we need to say yes and no or "no further" when that response is appropriate. When we fail to establish and enforce healthy limits and boundaries, we set ourselves up for far more hurt, far less trust, and far more anger down the road.

Where, if at all, do you step in where you're not wanted or needed?

Where, if at all, do you let others dictate your decisions and mood?

6. Anger is powerful.

One reason we're afraid of others' anger is that it feels overwhelming and intimidating. Their expression dominates us. But the right response to others' unhealthy anger is our own healthy anger. Instead of cowering in fear or lashing out in rage, we can use our powerful anger in constructive ways to move forward in speaking the truth, clarifying our points, setting limits and boundaries, and inviting our antagonists to have constructive conversations.

One reason many people are so angry so much of the time is that it gives them an adrenaline rush and makes them feel alive. Far too often, the energy is channeled in unhealthy ways, but it can be directed toward something good, right, and productive. Susan Jeffers writes,

> I remember times when my anger felt nothing short of sublime. It gave me a heady sense of power. It made leaving easier. It motivated me to make healthy changes in my life. It drove me to prove to everyone (especially myself) that I was competent and that I could do anything I wanted to do in life. Anger insidiously, but mercifully, masked the fear and pain and poison within.[6]

Anger can be a powerful fuel of forward progress.

Anger generates a lot of energy. What are some ways you can use it for good?

7. Healthy anger is learned.

Unhealthy anger comes naturally. Our parents didn't have us sit down so they could teach us how to mess up our lives with out-of-control or too-much-control expressions of anger. They did something far more important: they modeled it. Of course, some parents were "good enough" and modeled relatively healthy ways of expressing feelings of anger, but if you're reading this workbook, chances are that your parents or caregivers were on the other end of the spectrum.

James told me, "In some ways, I never knew what was coming. But in another way, I was always on edge because I knew my mom and dad would blow up soon . . . at each other, at me, at my sister, and at anything else they could think of." James came to see me because he had tried so hard to clamp down his intense feelings of anger, but it was spilling out onto his wife and toddler.

Rachel had a different experience, but with similar results: "I never saw my parents raise their voices or speak an unkind word. I thought they were the best in the world . . . but I had no idea what to do with my own emotional life. I eventually realized they'd modeled emotional repression, not emotional honesty."

If much of how we express our anger is learned, it can be unlearned, and healthy expressions of anger can be learned for the first time.

We'll spend much more time on this later in the book, but for now, describe the way your parents modeled unhealthy and/or healthy expressions of anger. What impact did their example have on you?

8. Anger is the emotion "most often mislabeled."

In recent years, it has become much more common for people, including Christians, to express grievance and outrage. Only a few years ago, most Christian women didn't feel the freedom to verbalize their anger because "good Christians don't get angry," but today, that's less the case. As we've seen, in many instances, visible anger is a reaction to an undercurrent of hurt, frustration, fear, and shame. But quite often, anger isn't visible—it masquerades as anxiety, depression, worry, or apathy.

In our book, *When Anger Hits Home*, Norm Wright and I observed:

> When we begrudge, scorn, insult, and disdain others or when we are annoyed, offended, bitter, fed up, repulsed, irritated, infuriated, incensed, mad, sarcastic, uptight, cross, or when we experience frustration, indignation, exasperation, fury, wrath, or rage, we are probably experiencing some form of anger. Anger can also manifest itself as criticism, silence, intimidation, hypochondria, numerous petty

> complaints, depression, gossip, sarcasm, and blame. Even such passive-aggressive behaviors as stubbornness, half-hearted efforts, forgetfulness, and laziness can be evidence of an angry spirit.[7]

Why the hurricane of so many words? Because so many of us insist we're not angry when we really are, so we excuse, minimize, or rationalize the anger in others because the truth is too much to bear.

Look back at the quote. Which of the words are better descriptions for your emotions than simply "anger"?

9. Anger is the emotion "most likely to be blamed."

Anger has a bad reputation, especially among Christians. If someone behaves in a way that makes us uncomfortable, we quickly make an assessment: "He's always mad," or "She's such an angry person!" Certainly, anger is a real problem for many people (or I wouldn't be writing this workbook!), but it's not the *only* problem . . . and it usually isn't the *primary* problem.

When the inner cauldron of grievances and fury continues to boil, we may feel more alive, but we harm everyone around us. When we feel empowered by our anger, we don't want to give it up, and when others are intimidated by our anger, they're reluctant to address it. It's easier to write it off, for us and them, as "no big deal," although there's far more going on under the surface.

For instance, *ire* suggests an intense emotion, often accompanied by flushed cheeks and dilated pupils. *Hostility* is the desire to lash out at the perceived offender (and possibly innocent bystanders) to punish and retaliate. *Aggression* is hostility put into action. *Rage* (like road rage) demands instant justice, and *hate* is a settled, steel-reinforced resentment. All these feelings go beyond the emotion of anger, and they certainly aren't directed toward the powerfully positive blend of truth and love.

What extreme expressions do you often see, in yourself or others, that are excused as "just anger"?

10. Mismanaged anger can be hazardous to your health.

In fact, it can kill you. Unresolved, unrelenting, unhealthy anger puts stress on the heart and can lead to heart disease. It increases stress hormones and keeps levels abnormally elevated. It raises the risk of Type 2 diabetes. It disrupts digestion, aggravates sleep problems, erodes the ability to concentrate, is associated with distractions that cause traffic accidents, and makes us more cynical and anxious. One of the most common definitions of depression is "anger turned inward." People who suffer from depression, mild or severe, often don't eat well, sleep well, think well, or take care of their physical needs.

Who do you know who has health problems that may be caused by unaddressed anger? What's the impact on that person's body?

For many of us, our perceptions about ourselves, others, God, and life seem so baked in that it's impossible to change, but that's not the case. Anger may be a problem today, but it can become a true blessing tomorrow. For that radical transformation to happen, we need to be honest and brave, and we need the support of people who can help us. We haven't explored all the causes and other factors that contribute to unhealthy anger, but it's wise to begin to look at some important steps forward. Take plenty of time to work through this exercise.

Make Anger Work FOR You

Like any other skill, managing anger takes practice. The next time you get angry, try some of these approaches:

- Write a clear and specific statement: I'm angry because ______________________________.
- Study this moment of anger. Make a list of reasons why you are so angry.
- Visualize being in the room with the person who has caused your anger. What would you say? Write a script with a clear first sentence to memorize and the rest in an outline, at least.
- Choose a time to talk that's good for you and the person. Maintain eye contact and a calm voice while talking.
- Put yourself in the other person's shoes. Allow yourself to be wrong some of the time.
- Avoid blaming, attacking, or bringing up other or old grievances. Keep your focus on the recent event.
- Use "I" statements, such as "I get angry when . . ." Avoid blaming statements that start with "you": "You always . . ." or "You never . . ."
- Can the situation be changed or avoided in the future? If the answer is yes, think about how that can happen. If the answer is no, work toward acceptance. Remember that you can't control others' behavior, but you can control how you respond.
- Use relaxation techniques such as deep breathing exercises or imagery, focusing on a peaceful place, thought, or sound. Find a physical outlet for your anger, such as exercise or housework.

- Write a letter to the person, but don't deliver it for a few days (if then). Then read it again and decide if you need to make changes to the message or the delivery.
- Use positive self-talk, such as, "I'm angry, but I can get on with my life."
- Set a time limit for anger. ("Don't let the sun go down on your anger.")

Keep track of your anger responses. Look back over the previous week and identify three or four instances when you got angry. For each one, fill in the chart.

Situation and Trigger	My Reaction	Something I Did Well	Something I Could Have Done Better

CHAPTER 3

THE SOURCES OF ANGER

When Charles and Alicia began telling me why they'd come for counseling, their differences were immediately evident. Charles crossed his arms and his legs—and he would have crossed his ears if he'd had that option. His body language yelled, "I don't want to be here!" Meanwhile, Alicia leaned toward me and poured her heart out. She was desperate to find a solution to their inability to communicate well.

I asked each of them to tell me about their childhoods. Charles rolled his eyes, but Alicia dove in. She explained, "My parents were very demonstrative—with their anger, their love, and everything in between. Nothing was off limits. They encouraged me to talk about my feelings, and they never condemned me for having them. I know our family wasn't perfect, but it was pretty wonderful."

I turned to Charles and waited for him to speak. He grimaced, but then he began, "Mine, not so much. My father was an alcoholic, the loud and angry kind. My mother was terrified of him when he was drunk and really kind to him when he was sober. My brother and I tried to find our place in all this. We turned out all right, I guess."

I didn't want to let him off so easily, so I asked, "How did you and your brother try to find your place?"

Charles thought for a few seconds, and then he said, "Actually, we went in two very different directions. My brother was 'the good kid,' always trying to protect Mom from Dad, comforting her when she cried, which was a lot, and being there for her morning, noon, and night. That didn't work for me. It seemed weak . . . dependent. I was too mad at Dad for being a lousy father, I was mad at Mom for letting him get away with it, and I was mad at my brother for sucking up to her."

"Tell me more about your anger," I prodded.

Charles laughed and sat back in his chair. "Oh, I've got stories. I broke stuff in the house, wrecked our car a couple of times, burned some of my brother's favorite albums, and left home as soon as I turned 18. You know, normal stuff."

Yes, sadly, "normal" for a lot of people.

In this chapter, we'll examine a number of factors that contribute to our sense of being threatened and our reactions and responses to those threats.

Childhood Experiences

As I mentioned earlier, we don't need perfect parents, but we desperately need "good enough" parents, the kind who are emotionally present, sufficiently affirming, and who lovingly correct us when we need it. Alicia had parents like that; Charles didn't. When children don't have good role models, they don't learn how to process and express their thoughts and feelings. When that happens, some become rebels like Charles, some withdraw into a shell to protect themselves from being hurt again, some try to dominate people to be "one up," and others are so desperate to find a place and earn approval that they read people's expressions so they can adapt their behavior, hoping to please them. In other words, there's not a cookie-cutter reaction to "not-good-enough" parenting.

How do you think the nature of your relationship with your parents affected your emotional life?

Physiological Needs

Poor health erodes our ability to respond to difficulties. How many of us "snap" at those we love when we're sick? Some of us live with chronic illness or pain, which saps our physical and emotional energy. When I meet with new clients, and especially someone who has come to deal with anger, I do a quick lifestyle check. I ask questions like:

- How is your health? When was your last complete physical?
- What kind of regular exercise do you get?
- How is your nutrition? What did you have for breakfast this morning?
- Do you have any problems going to sleep? Staying asleep? Getting up in the morning?
- What's your schedule for an average work week?
- How much time do spend recovering from a stressful day?
- How much quality time do you spend with your spouse? And your kids?

Okay, it's your turn. Answer these questions. What do your answers tell you about your health status?

Unrelieved Stress

"I'm running on empty," Philip told me. "When I get home, I don't have any reserves for my family." Like many people in our hectic, driven world, Philip had pushed himself to the brink of burnout, and it affected every aspect of his life.

Quite often, anger flares over something relatively minor. If it happened only once or very rarely, it wouldn't be a big deal, but if the husband leaves the toilet seat up for the eighth time this week, the boy leaves his bike in the driveway for three days in a row, the wife interrupts her husband over and over while he watches his favorite team, or the girl forgets to do her homework yet again, one minor event can be "the straw that breaks the camel's back," and anger erupts.

Over time, little annoyances accumulate. I don't like to be interrupted when I'm focused on writing a talk or a chapter of a book. When an "urgent call" breaks my concentration, it irritates me a little bit. If people walk in and interrupt to ask a question two or three times within an hour or so,

I get frustrated because I lose my train of thought . . . and I never know if I'll get it back as clearly. If I'm tired and weary, I'm even more vulnerable. With each interruption, my fuse gets a little shorter, and woe to the unsuspecting person who is Interruption #5!

Do you get upset over "little things"? If so, what are the last two or three you can remember? Can you identify a sequence of events that led up to that moment?

Injustice

God wired every human being (except, perhaps, sociopaths!) with a moral compass. We have an innate longing for justice, and we react to any perceived threat to justice because injustice is a violation of a person's dignity and rights. Throughout history, we find courageous people who championed victims of injustice, including Abraham Lincoln, Martin Luther King, Jr., and of course, Jesus. Again and again in the Gospels, we see Jesus standing against the rigidity and callousness of the religious leaders to heal lepers, restore sight, heal the lame, and love the lost and the least. Throughout the Bible, we see that God loves justice and hates injustice. For instance, Isaiah quotes God:

> For I the Lord love justice;
> I hate robbery and wrong;
> I will faithfully give them their recompense,
> and I will make an everlasting covenant with them. (Isaiah 61:8)

In Mark's Gospel, Jesus entered a synagogue on a Sabbath and noticed a man with a withered hand. He invited the man to approach him. The religious leaders were watching closely to see if Jesus would have the audacity to heal someone on the Sabbath, which they considered to be a terrible sin. With the man standing in front of him, Jesus asked those self-righteous leaders, "Is it lawful on the Sabbath to do good or to do harm, to save life or to kill?" In other words, "You don't get it! You don't understand the meaning of justice. You think it's more important to follow your interpretation of the Law than to follow God's command to love your neighbor." In response, the leaders were silent. Mark tells us:

> He looked around at them with anger, grieved at their hardness of heart, and said to the man, "Stretch out your hand." He stretched it out, and his hand was restored. The Pharisees went out and immediately held counsel with the Herodians against him, how to destroy him. (Mark 3:5-6)

Here's an example of Jesus feeling anger toward one group of people while responding with love and empathy for a hurting person. Virtually everyone reading this workbook will have suffered injustice, some quite severe, others not as bad, and it's perfectly good and right to be angry as a result. As we've seen and will see many more times in these pages, we have the choice to react or respond, to lash out or suppress the powerful emotions . . . or to channel them to stand up and speak up for victims, including ourselves.

What injustices have you suffered? How have you reacted in the past? How might you respond in a more healthy, productive way?

The Inner Critic

Many of us have audio loops playing in our heads. They're loud, harsh, and persistent—and the self-condemnation seems to make perfect sense. We are, in fact, our own worst critics. The voice we hear focuses on our failures and flaws: real ones, perceived ones, and the dread of future ones. The criticism may be accompanied by flashbacks of painful events and hateful words that make us feel weak and vulnerable. We might believe, cognitively, that God considers us loved, forgiven, accepted, and a delight. But feelings frequently override those thoughts, and we call ourselves names: "stupid," "fool," "can't do anything right," "worthless," "helpless," and "less than." Such messages erode our self-concept and leave us feeling deeply ashamed and fragile. In this condition (and many of us are in this condition most of the time), anger seethes just below the surface, ready to erupt at any moment.

The term *inner critic* was coined by Pete Walker in his book on complex PTSD. In an article on his website, he explains:

> In my work with clients repetitively traumatized in childhood, I am continuously struck by how frequently the various thought processes of the inner critic trigger them into overwhelming emotional flashbacks. This is because the PTSD-derived inner critic weds shame and self-hate about imperfection to fear of abandonment, and mercilessly drive the psyche with the entwined serpents of perfectionism and endangerment. Recovering individuals must learn to recognize, confront and disidentify from the many inner critic processes that tumble them back in emotional time to the awful feelings of overwhelming fear, self-hate, hopelessness and self-disgust that were part and parcel of their original childhood abandonment.[8]

What names do you call yourself? How would you describe the cumulative effect of these messages up to this point in your life?

Where do you think the voice of your inner critic came from? Who does it sound like?

Worry

There's nothing wrong with being observant, analytical, and concerned. That's how emotionally healthy people navigate life. But worry is concern that has gone too far. It focuses on the "what ifs" and "if onlys." The "what ifs" are fears about what might happen, and the "if onlys" are regrets about what already happened.

In the Lord's Prayer, Jesus taught us to pray, "Your kingdom come, your will be done, on earth as it is in heaven" (Matthew 6:10). This part of the prayer taps into our highest and best desire as well as our willingness to submit to God's will. When we pray, "Your kingdom come," we're asking God to expand our network of kindness for the hurting, justice for the oppressed, and the rule of Jesus, our righteous king. When we pray, "Your will be done," we're saying, "Lord, I accept whatever you send my way, the good and the bad, because you've promised to use everything for good in my life. I trust in you."

Worried people don't pray this prayer, or if they do, they don't mean it. Worry indicates, "God, I know better than you how my life should go, and you're messing things up!" This exasperation multiplies our regrets of the past and our fears of the future, and it robs us of peace and trust in the present. Consequently, we live with a chip on our shoulders, always defensive, with a hair-trigger on our anger. We're convinced we deserve better, and we become sour and cynical.

Do you agree or disagree that worry is based on the belief that we know better than God how our lives should go? Explain your answer.

Conflict

Some of us are so afraid of conflict that we give in to any demands, even those that aren't even verbalized. In many families and offices, conflict (or the possibility of it) is a way of life. Some people thrive on conflict because they've developed the skills to win almost every argument, but many others avoid it at all costs—they give in, withdraw, or try to become invisible. Give-and-take of different views can be very healthy and stimulating, but that's not what I'm talking about here. Avoiding conflict isn't healthy, and it doesn't leave people feeling inspired. In these environments, people learn to live with their defenses always up, like it's an armed truce and they're expecting someone to cross the line at any moment. One of the most important skills we can learn is to disagree agreeably.

What kind of conflict did your family experience when you were a child? How did you react?

How healthy or unhealthy are your conflicts now? (We all have them!)

Fear

Fear doesn't look or feel like anger, but the two are inextricably linked. We've said that anger is aroused when we feel threatened, and being threatened is at the heart of fear. On the surface, people may be afraid of snakes, spiders, heights, tight spaces, and other critters or conditions, but more debilitating fears center on the threat of humiliation, rejection, failure, being found out, being abandoned, or losing control. In Chapter 4, we'll explore fear as a source of anger more fully, but for now, know that expressions of anger are often ways people mask their fears. Fear makes them feel weak and vulnerable, but anger makes them feel strong.

How would you describe the connection between fear and anger? Is it possible that at least some of your expressions of anger are ways you mask your fear?

Hurt

Many people carry crushing memories of a painful past their entire lives, and they don't realize how the unhealed hurts affect every aspect of their existence. Hurt, like fear, makes us feel uncomfortable and vulnerable. We don't like feeling that way, so we use anger as a substitute. Hurt inevitably produces anger, but expressions of anger vary widely. As we've seen, some of us get strong and tough as we determine, *No one is ever going to hurt me again!* Others feel threatened by their emotional pain and the possibility that, in their expression of anger, they may appear to be out of control, so they repress their anger and live in a toxic, private, lonely world of pain, fear, and resentment. They have internalized the belief: *If no one gets close to me, no one can hurt me.* Still others seek escapes from the intense hurt they've suffered. They use substances to numb the pain or behaviors like pornography, adultery, gambling, shopping, working long hours, or some other diversion to keep from feeling it.

Would those who know you best say that your anger is masking some deep emotional pain? Would you agree with them?

Assessment

Take some time to reflect on the various factors that contribute to your anger. Rate each one on a scale of 0 (not in the least) to 10 (all day every day).

Childhood experiences	0	1	2	3	4	5	6	7	8	9	10
Physiological needs	0	1	2	3	4	5	6	7	8	9	10
Unrelieved stress	0	1	2	3	4	5	6	7	8	9	10
Injustice	0	1	2	3	4	5	6	7	8	9	10
The inner critic	0	1	2	3	4	5	6	7	8	9	10
Worry	0	1	2	3	4	5	6	7	8	9	10
Conflict	0	1	2	3	4	5	6	7	8	9	10
Fear	0	1	2	3	4	5	6	7	8	9	10
Hurt	0	1	2	3	4	5	6	7	8	9	10

Which are your top three?

Were any of these a surprise? If so, which ones?

All in Your Head

God has created us so we can react quickly to danger. This ability was really important when sabertoothed tigers lurked in the bushes, and today, it's one of God's great gifts we can put into action in an emergency. Near our temples are two small parts of the brain called the amygdala. Some people call it "the reptile brain" because it ignites primitive defenses to protect us when we feel threatened. In a nanosecond, hormones flood our bodies, making us instantly more alert, stronger, and quicker. In an accident or an attack, our "rational brain" is immediately overwhelmed by our primitive brain. That's why we sometimes hear people say, "I was so upset I couldn't even think!" They're speaking the honest truth.

Problems can arise, however, when we perceive we're being threatened when we're not. In response, we instinctively react to defend ourselves (we *fight*), we leave the room (we *flee*), or we become emotionally and mentally immobilized (we *freeze*). This is called "amygdala hijacking." One client told me, "Most people see me as a thoughtful, rational person, but when my wife flies off the handle and yells at me, something happens and I become mush-brained. I can't think, I can't argue, I can't defend, and I can't think of anything to do but stand there and take it. I know that's not good for either of us, but I feel helpless to do anything else."

Psychiatrist Bessel Van Der Kolk calls the amygdala the brain's "smoke detector."[9] When it senses a threat, it sounds an alarm to trigger an emergency response. Before we have a coherent thought, the amygdala releases chemicals, including adrenaline and cortisol, to equip us to fight or flee, but some of us are so immobilized that we freeze. In an article in the *Harvard Business Review*, Diane Hamilton describes how perceived threats "trigger" us to react. She explains:

> The active amygdala also immediately shuts down the neural pathway to our prefrontal cortex so we can become disoriented in a heated conversation. Complex decision-making disappears, as does our access to multiple perspectives. As our attention narrows, we find ourselves trapped in the one perspective that makes us feel the most safe: "I'm right and you're wrong," even though we ordinarily see more perspectives.
>
> And if that wasn't enough, our memory becomes untrustworthy. Have you ever been in a fight with your partner or friend, and you literally can't remember a positive thing about them? It's as though the brain drops the memory function altogether in an effort to survive the threat. When our memory is compromised like this, we can't recall something from the past that might help us calm down. In fact, we can't remember much of anything. Instead, we're simply filled with the flashing red light of the amygdala indicating "Danger, react. Danger, protect. Danger, attack."[10]

During such moments, we're overwhelmed with emotions. This experience is called "flooding," which is "a sensation of feeling psychologically and physically overwhelmed during conflict, making it virtually impossible to have a productive, problem-solving discussion."[11] Daniel Goleman, author of *Emotional Intelligence*, explains that our childhood experiences affect the way our brains function today:

> [Emotional memories created by abuse or neglect] are established before infants have words for their experience . . . when these emotional memories are triggered in later life there is no matching set of articulated thoughts about the response that

> takes us over. One reason we can be so baffled by our emotional outbursts, then, is that they often date from a time early in our lives when things were bewildering, and we did not yet have words for comprehending events. We may have the chaotic feelings, but not the words for the memories that formed them.[12]

Have you wondered where your emotional outbursts come from? This may be the answer to your question. One of the problems is generational transmission. When a parent experiences amygdala hijacking on a regular basis, it certainly is difficult to make sense of it, but it also creates a sense of insecurity and confusion in the rest of the family, which may then be replicated in the next generation—like yours. The specific unhealthy behavior as a reaction to insecurity may not be exactly the same from one generation to another, but until someone breaks the cycle, the *degree* of dysfunction is the same. For instance, James told me his father was violent sometimes and emotionally distant the rest of the time. James felt unloved and unsafe as a child. As a dad, he was determined not to replicate his father's behavior. Instead, he smothered his children with attention and directions, taking responsibility for their decisions until they left home. He overcompensated. He didn't do what his dad did, but his impact was just as unhealthy.

How would you describe "amygdala hijacking"?

When does that happen to you? How do you react?

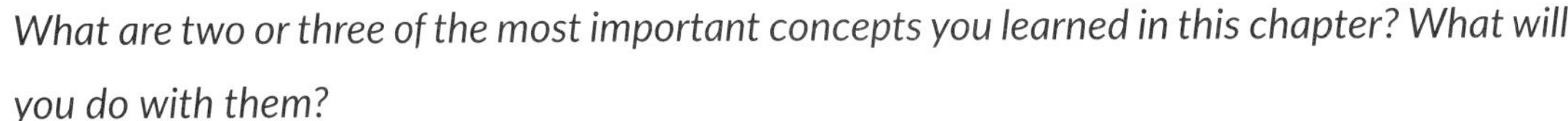

What are two or three of the most important concepts you learned in this chapter? What will you do with them?

In the next three chapters, we'll look at three primary causes of the secondary emotion of anger: past hurts, present frustrations, and fears of the future.

CHAPTER 4

HURT: PAST MEMORIES AND WOUNDS

Jackie dispassionately shared with the therapy group about her childhood. She talked about her perfectionist mother and her emotionally distant father. "Nothing I ever did was good enough for her, and when I needed love and support the most, Dad found something else to do. He watched a lot of television." Jackie laughed, "I don't really blame him. I'm sure Mom was just as demanding with him as she was with me!" She had suffered two very different kinds of wounds: emotional abuse from her mother and emotional abandonment by her father. "But it was even worse than that," she continued. "My younger sister was beautiful, and in Mom's eyes, she could do no wrong."

"Tell us about how you felt about each of them," the counselor said.

"Felt. That's a hard one for me," Jackie stammered. "I've spent most of my life avoiding my feelings." She paused, not knowing what to say next.

The counselor asked, "What do you mean? Tell us more about that."

No words came for a few seconds, and then tears began to flow down Jackie's cheeks. "I . . . I . . . I can't really say I haven't had any emotions, but I couldn't let them out in my house when I was a child. But, oh, they came out when I got married and had children! I've been a horrible mother . . . just horrible. I've unconsciously treated my older daughter the way my mother treated me—nothing was good enough. She's a bright and lovely person, but I found fault with anything and everything she did. And when she didn't please me enough, my temper blew up! The first time that happened, I was shocked. I had no idea that much anger was inside me. But it didn't stop for years and years."

The counselor asked, "When you think about your parents and your sister now, what memories come to mind?"

More tears. "My mother's face scowling at me. Her fury when I made an A minus in biology in high school. My dad walked away and sat alone. And my sister . . . I know I shouldn't hate her, but . . ."

Misguided Conclusions

We've said that one of the sources of anger is injustice, and abuse is patently unjust. Two experts explain, "Abuse is any behavior that is designed to control and/or subjugate another person through the use of fear, humiliation and verbal or physical assaults. In a sense, it is the systematic persecution of one family member by another."[13]

Abuse can take many different forms: verbal, emotional, and sexual. Some of us suffered physical or sexual violence, and our sense of safety was shattered. How many of these traumatic occasions does it take to do damage? Just one, but many have suffered multiple instances. Others, like Jackie, endured continuous verbal wounds. We weren't good enough, smart enough, handsome or pretty enough, or skilled enough to measure up to the people who counted. This kind of abuse (and yes, it's abuse) doesn't shatter us like a sledgehammer hitting a tile; it's more like sandpaper eroding our confidence, our security, and our hope for love and meaning. Sledgehammers and sandpaper both cause a lot of damage. They aren't just threats of injustice; they *are* injustice.

One of the primary impacts of an abuser is to warp the perception of the victim so they believe it's somehow their fault. The modern term for this is "gaslighting," which is a nod to a film by that title in which the villain caused the victim to believe she had lost her mind. Psychotherapist Beverly Engel describes it this way: "With emotional abuse, the insults, insinuations, criticism, and accusations slowly eat away at the victim's self-esteem until he or she is incapable of judging a situation realistically. He or she may begin to believe that there is something wrong with them or even fear they are losing their mind. They have become so beaten down emotionally that they blame themselves for the abuse."[14]

Survivors of abuse often tell themselves (and those they confide in):

- "I deserved it."
- "What's wrong with me?"

- "I'm damaged goods now."
- "No one would believe me if I told them."
- "We just need one more try to make it work."
- "I know he/she really loves me."
- "It'll be better tomorrow."

What are some reasons gaslighting is so effective?

Hurt and Anger

Let's go back to the therapy group and listen again to Jackie. The counselor asked, "Tell us how you felt about yourself when all that was happening."

"Oh, I thought my mother was perfect and my dad was the best father in the world. And my sister . . . I wished I could be just like her!"

"What changed your perceptions?"

"I finally realized what a fool I'd been to believe they were perfect and I was the entire problem. I'd like to say it happened as soon as I left home, or when I graduated from college, or when I got married, but it took longer than that. I couldn't face my own wounds until I saw how I was wounding my daughter."

"What emotions did you need to deal with?"

Jackie took a deep breath before she said, "A lot! I cried for hours every day for a month. When that started to subside, I became furious! One day, I thought I was going to explode. I drove to the country, got out of my car, and screamed. I won't tell you what I yelled. It wasn't pretty."

Jackie had finally realized she had bottled up her emotions—all of them, but especially her deep hurt and fierce anger. For years during her childhood and even as a married woman, she hadn't felt safe enough to let them out. When she did, it was under the care of a counselor who gave her permission to feel everything . . . without a hint of condemnation or correction.

"I didn't say anything all those years," Jackie explained, "because I didn't feel safe at home, and as an adult, I was afraid of coming unglued. The anger was there all along."

Broadly speaking, men are usually more aware of their anger than their emotional hurts, and women are usually more in touch with their hurt than their anger. That statement was more true a decade or two ago, but it still holds true in many cases. Of course, I've known a number of sensitive, perceptive men who were well aware of their deep wounds when they walked into my office for the first time, and I've seen displays of the wrath of women more times than I can count. The principle is to "start with what you've got." If you're more in tune with your anger, realize it's a secondary emotion that's driven by molten lava beneath the surface. Or if you're more aware of the primary emotion of hurt, you may still need to do some work to uncover the secondary anger that was taboo to express when you were a child, and that still frightens you today.

Peeling Back the Layers

Memories are powerful, but they can be elusive. Those who have suffered significant abuse may dissociate and are no longer aware of the events (or at least the worst ones) that caused their pain.

In the next day or so, carve out an hour to be alone . . . really alone. Turn your phone off and sit quietly with a pen and a notebook. Ask God to bring to mind the events that have caused you pain, and write them down. Most people can quickly identify ten or twelve events.

After you record enough detail to recall what you felt—or could have felt—at the time, be quiet again and be open to other memories. Many people will remember events they haven't thought about in a long time. Write these down, and then be open again. Ten, twenty, or thirty minutes may pass when nothing comes to mind, and then you may remember something you hadn't thought about in many years. It may seem insignificant or irrelevant, but it's probably not, so write it down.

In your next counseling session or group meeting, share the most important stories and enter into the emotions you felt as you remembered them.

The Necessity of Grief

Many people assume that grief applies to those who have died. It does, but it's much broader than that. We need to grieve every significant loss, and those who have been emotionally wounded have suffered staggering losses. They've lost their sense of safety and security, their hope to be loved by their parents and siblings, their joy and happiness, their innocence, their ability to process difficulties, and many other vital aspects of life. Grief is an essential part of healing from the wounds you identified in the previous exercise. They aren't just historical events in a dusty book; those memories are about people who treated you with contempt, and that hurts a lot.

For decades, experts in the psychology of grief have taught that grieving is not linear. People take one step forward, then two down a dead-end trail, and one backward before they take another step forward. In the process, they come to grips with the depth and breadth of the losses and the consequences they've suffered. If they try to rush the process and prematurely insist it's over, fresh grief is likely to hit like a hammer a week or a month later. Like the healing of a broken bone, the process of grief takes time and attention. Eventually, however, the pain subsides, confidence grows, and hope replaces despair.

How is grieving past wounds like and unlike grieving the death of someone we love?

What are some reasons why processing grief is necessary to emotional healing?

The Empty Chair and Letters

A very helpful practice for those struggling with emotional wounds is "the empty chair." It may be too dangerous to have a face-to-face conversation with an abuser, or dialogue may not be possible because the offender has died or been sentenced to prison. In such cases, you can have an imaginary conversation with the person who is "sitting in the empty chair." You can say things you wish you could have said but didn't feel safe enough; you can articulate what you wish the relationship had been but wasn't; and you can share how the person has shattered or eroded your sense of safety and hope.

It's most helpful if you do this with a counselor or in a group. Whenever and however you do it, be sure to take plenty of time to process what you thought and felt during the "conversation."

Another technique to help you become more objective about the pain is to write letters to the people who hurt you . . . but don't send them. You can say what you need to say about the abuse and the damage the person caused. Be specific, and use whatever words you're feeling. You might also consider writing a letter ostensibly from that person to you, expressing all you wish had been expressed to you over the years. This letter may help you uncover your losses more specifically.

How might an empty chair or writing a letter help you grieve and heal your hurts?

Two Mistakes

Forgiveness is both an act and a process. Most people make one of two mistakes in response to those who have hurt them: they forgive too soon or they forgive too late.

Conscientious Christians may have been taught to forgive "completely and immediately," which is bad advice. It appears to resolve the offence quickly, but the forgiveness is usually incomplete. The pain and anger tend to resurface sooner or later, and the person wonders, *What happened? Why didn't forgiveness free me completely, all at once?* We can choose to forgive an offender as much as we can and as soon as we can, but that initial act of forgiveness must be followed by an ongoing process that requires significant time and attention.

Many others are on the other end of the spectrum: they forgive too late, meaning not at all. Resentment and bitterness are forms of anger that feel good, but eat us alive. Pastor Frederick Buechner observed, "Of the Seven Deadly Sins, anger is possibly the most fun. To lick your wounds, to smack your lips over grievances long past, to roll over your tongue the prospect of bitter confrontations still to come, to savor to the last toothsome morsel both the pain you are given and the pain you are giving back—in many ways it is a feast fit for a king. The chief drawback is that what you are wolfing down is yourself. The skeleton at the feast is you!"[15]

When we shake our heads and say, "Oh, it didn't really bother me that much," we're blocking the process of forgiveness and we stay stuck in the prison of our pain. You may have been taught to just "let it go," but that's not forgiveness either. Professor Lewis Smedes wrote with piercing insight about this topic. He explained the need to be objective: "When we forgive evil we do not excuse it, we do not tolerate it, we do not smother it. We look the evil full in the face, call it what it is, let its horror shock and stun and enrage us, and only then do we forgive it."[16]

Bitterness gives us two things we desperately want: identity and energy. We can claim to be "the one who was wronged," which gives us an excuse to lash out, withdraw, give people the silent treatment, or use our words to tear them down. Yet bitterness is a prison for our souls. Smedes observed, "Vengeance is having a videotape planted in your soul that cannot be turned off. It plays the painful scene over and over again inside your mind . . . And each time it plays you feel the clap of pain again . . . Forgiving turns off the videotape of pained memory. Forgiving sets you free."[17]

In his letter to the Romans, Paul gave clear directions about the dangers of taking revenge on those who have hurt us:

> Repay no one evil for evil, but give thought to do what is honorable in the sight of all. If possible, so far as it depends on you, live peaceably with all. Beloved, never avenge yourselves, but leave it to the wrath of God, for it is written, "Vengeance is mine, I will repay, says the Lord." (Romans 12:17-19)

A friend told me that this passage changed his perspective about forgiving his abusive father and passive mother. He related, "For years—decades, really—I refused to forgive them because it seemed totally unfair to let them completely off the hook. I lived in bitterness all this time . . . and I'm a Christian! But when I understood this passage, I realized that I could take them off my hook because they were still on God's hook. When I thought justice was up to me, I couldn't forgive. When I realized I could put them in God's hands, I could forgive them. The question was: Could I trust God to be fair and just with them? I decided I could."

When anger, even healthy anger, isn't addressed, it can quickly turn into something destructive and consuming. Frederick Buechner warned:

> Hate is as all-absorbing as love, as irrational, and in its own way as satisfying. As lovers thrive on the presence of the beloved, haters revel in encounters with the one they hate. They confirm him in all his darkest suspicions. They add fuel to all his most burning animosities. The anticipation of them makes the hating heart pound. The memory of them can be as sweet as young love. The major difference between hating and loving is perhaps that whereas to love somebody is to be fulfilled and enriched by the experience, to hate somebody is to be diminished and drained by it. Lovers, by losing themselves in their loving, find themselves, become themselves. Haters simply lose themselves. Theirs is the ultimately consuming passion.[18]

How would you describe the benefits of bitterness? What damage does it do?

How does it help to realize forgiveness is both an event and a process?

Setting Boundaries

"I don't want to rock the boat."

"If I say anything, it will only get worse."

"He promised it wouldn't happen again."

"I think it's out of her system."

"It won't work. Nothing works."

These are just a few of the imaginative ways people avoid being honest with those who continue to hurt them. They often call it love, but it's anything but that . . . it's paralyzing fear. Earlier, we mentioned the need to set limits ("This is as far as I'm willing to go") and boundaries ("This is as far as I'm willing for you to go"). Now, let's be more specific. If someone regularly hurts you, it's even more essential that you set limits and boundaries, clearly articulate the consequences of crossing them, and enforce them.

If you fail to enforce your limits and boundaries (by minimizing, excusing, rationalizing, or denying the problem), you communicate to the other person in all caps: YOU'LL PAY NO PRICE FOR CONTINUING TO HURT ME! Remember, passive people have plenty of anger; they just shove it down into their souls because it's too uncomfortable, and they don't want to take the risk of being blasted by the overtly angry person. When you begin to get in touch with the hurt, your anger will be validated, and your newfound anger can be a powerful fuel to propel a healthy and mature response.

If you're someone who uses any and all forms of anger to manipulate, intimidate, and control, your path is similar in some ways, but different in others. You'll need to set limits on your expressions of anger, but instead of setting boundaries for yourself, you'll need to invite the other person (or people) to set and enforce boundaries.

Let's look at some limits you might need to set, first as the survivor of another's anger:

1. Be objective about the manipulation and intimidation you've experienced. You've probably spent years downplaying it; now it's time to be honest. You'll likely need plenty of help as you gradually begin to comprehend the extent of the damage done. Get professional help from a counselor and perhaps an attorney, especially if you're facing an ongoing physical threat.

2. If necessary, get away from the threatening person and stay away as long as it takes to be in a safe place.

3. If a physical threat isn't an issue, with the help of a counselor, determine what you want in your relationship with the angry abuser. This is often harder than it first seems. People spend years lowering their standards of what's acceptable in this difficult relationship, so they may have trouble even thinking about expecting communication based on trust and respect. But that needs to be the new non-negotiable requirement! Nothing less will do, and there will be consequences for crossing that line.

4. Shift the responsibility. Stop asking yourself (a zillion times), *What's wrong with me, that I deserve this kind of abuse?* Instead, ask, *What's wrong with him (or her), that intimidation seems not only permissible, but desirable?*

5. Write a script of what you want to say. Keep it short, and make the boundaries clear. I always recommend including the statement: "I want a relationship based on trust and respect," followed by a definition of the boundaries and the consequences of breaching them. Write it all out, memorize at least the first statement, and keep the script or outline in your hand as you talk. Remember the amygdala hijacking? It can happen as you face the abuser, and your mind can go numb. Fight this reaction with a clear script . . . and perhaps the borrowed courage of your counselor or sponsor.

6. Be specific. In your preparation, you may think of a dozen things you could say, but choose no more than three, such as:

   "I won't permit you to swear at me."

   "I won't permit you to yell at me."

   "I won't permit you to use your anger to intimidate and manipulate me."

   Communicate the boundaries and consequences. "If you do this, here's what I'll do."

7. Practice, practice, practice. Let's be honest: most of us come to this point with no experience and a ton of terror. In any new activity (piano lessons, learning a new language, etc.), there's a learning curve. You can flatten the curve by going over your script and perhaps using the empty chair in the presence of your counselor or group.

8. Have realistic expectations of the conversation. Your preparations will give you insight and courage to follow through with the script, but you can count on it being somewhat

awkward and difficult. Don't let yourself get caught up in a long explanation of your points. That's another way the person wants to control you! Have a good exit strategy, and end the conversation on your terms.

9. Debrief with your counselor or group. You'll undoubtedly have a lot of conflicting emotions, so take time to process them. You'll need to do this again, you know!

10. Follow through with the consequences. This is new territory for you, so be prepared. Again, write a script, have a short but pointed conversation, and enforce your boundaries. You'll probably need to do this a number of times to convince the person you really mean it. (But of course, if you're in physical danger, the police and the courts will enforce the boundaries.)

If you're the survivor, what are your thoughts and feelings as you read about these steps I'm suggesting you take?

Who can help you?

If you're the one who uses anger to manipulate and control:

1. Take responsibility. No more excusing your behavior; no more saying, "Everybody does it," or "It wasn't that bad." Own it . . . all of it.
2. Give the survivor plenty of space to describe the pain you've caused. Don't correct or minimize. Listen and affirm. This is crucial.
3. Apologize. If your apology isn't genuine, it will take the relationship backward.
4. Accept the boundaries and consequences. If you fight back, you'll show that you aren't willing to admit your wrong words and actions.
5. Enter a process of healing. For reconciliation to happen, you need to communicate and follow through with three things: (1) your apology needs to be genuine, and repeated as often as it takes; (2) you need to enter into the survivor's grief and loss . . . because you caused it; and (3) you need to show that you won't act that way again. These results won't be accomplished in a single conversation. The wound was caused over time, and healing will take time as well . . . but it's not just the passage of time that matters. Healing and reconciliation require real change, living by the person's boundaries, and getting a grip on the cause of your manipulative anger so you can change from the inside out.

If you're the one who has used anger to manipulate and dominate, what are your thoughts and feelings as you read the process I'm suggesting for you?

Who can help you?

Does this sound like a lot of work for both people? It should, because it is. Short-term, it's not easy, but in the long run, it's a lot easier than stuffing, repressing, suppressing, denying, and ignoring the problem. It's the only pathway that leads to change, growth, and personal and relational health. I've had the honor of being in the room with thousands of people—couples, parents and children, siblings—who were amazingly brave as they learned to speak the truth in love, enter this process of healing deep wounds, and see genuine love replace anger and fear in their relationships. It can happen. Trust me, I've seen it.

CHAPTER 5

FRUSTRATION: PRESENT BUTTONS AND IRRITATIONS

Anger often begins as frustration—a minor irritant, yet an unwelcome entry into our day. On closer inspection, we see that frustration is caused by anything that blocks the fulfillment of a desire or need. Even little things can threaten our sense of autonomy (control over ourselves, situations, and people) and make us feel dissatisfied.

Much anger is a reaction to what's happening today . . . right now! We're stuck in traffic and late for an appointment; we're ready to leave the office, but the boss calls a meeting; the toddler drew on the sofa with lipstick; and you hit your golf shot into the water . . . again. The list of frustrations is endless. One guy told me that one of his biggest frustrations is that when he looks at his lawn, all he sees are the weeds. (I've seen his yard, and believe me, he has very few weeds.)

And speaking of weeds . . . those of us who work in an office or in the service sector don't likely have hands calloused from hard physical labor. So, when we become weekend yard warriors and pick up a shovel or rake, in short order we might notice a burning sensation on a palm or the inside of a thumb: a blister resulting from a minor irritation that wasn't adequately addressed in time. We realize, too late, that we should have put on gloves (or enlisted a teenager to do the work for us). Lack of attention to our minor irritations (including our frustrations) means we pay a price. Sometimes the price is only tenderness, or maybe a popped blister and the need to wear a bandage for a while. All in all, that's no big deal. But many blisters and more significant frustrations can be avoided with a little preparation.

What are some frustrations you've experienced in the past week?

How did you react or respond to them?

Of course, people who've wrestled with deep hurts (see the previous chapter) already have thin emotional margins, so frustrations trigger a reaction much worse than getting a blister. They live in a tank of gasoline, and even a little spark nearby can ignite an explosion! Unresolved, unhealed emotional wounds from the past inevitably affect our ability to handle today's relatively minor frustrations. The principle is this: When a person's reaction is disproportionate to the event, there's something going on under the surface.

What are some examples of "disproportionate reactions" to minor events in your life?

The Family: Perfect Conditions for Frustrations

Now, let's get real . . . painfully real. Most of our frustrations involve the people who are closest to us: our spouse and children. Oh, sure, we get annoyed at work, with friends, in traffic, at restaurants, and everywhere else we go, but that's nothing compared to the amount of frustration with the people who live under our roofs!

Brad and Lacy had been married for about five years when they came to see me. They explained that the "little differences" that had seemed cute when they first married had, over the years, become sources of friction. Lacy looked exhausted as she told me, "I was so in love that I thought his lack of communication was normal, even manly. But that didn't last long. He doesn't listen, he doesn't talk, and he acts like everything is just fine . . . when it certainly isn't!" (I noticed she didn't call Brad by name.)

I nodded to Brad to invite him to respond. He just shrugged and mumbled, "I don't know what she wants from me. We were fine for a long time. Now she's getting on my nerves."

We had a lot to talk about over the next few weeks.

We could fill pages of potential flashpoints in marriage, but let's start with a representative list from both sides of the gender divide.

A woman can become annoyed when her husband or boyfriend . . .

- Pays more attention to his phone than to her.
- Forgets special dates and milestones.
- Insists on controlling the remote.
- Mumbles, "I don't care," when asked a question.
- Never apologizes.
- Takes her for granted.
- Seems more excited about spending time with friends than with her.
- Makes jokes to deflect a serious conversation.
- Doesn't ask about her day.
- Blames her for everything that goes wrong.
- Stares at other women's figures.

A man can become annoyed when his wife or girlfriend . . .

- Nags about, well, anything and everything.
- Interrupts a favorite show or sportscast.
- Says, "I'm fine," when she obviously isn't.
- Acts like his mother.
- Is too needy.
- Compares him to other men (especially her exes).
- Wants to know everything.
- Talks too much.
- Expects him to read her mind.
- Disagrees with him in public.
- Texts him about every detail of her life during the day.

These and many other complaints (I'm sure most readers can add to the list!) aren't a big deal if they happen only once in a long while, but they become significant friction points when they're frequent in a relationship. Some of the most common sources of marital conflict are:

- Money—Husbands and wives often have very different views of how to manage, save, and spend their financial resources;
- Sex—They often have different sexual desires;
- In-laws—The in-laws can be a great blessing or become hand grenades, blowing up the tranquility of the home; and
- Children—Parents often have very different methods of motivation and accountability. The struggles of parenting—and co-parenting with a spouse who has different views—change as children go through the stages of development. The exhaustion of tending to a newborn is a distant memory for parents of teenagers who are beginning to test the boundaries of authority. It's easy to become exasperated . . . with the child and the spouse . . . and live with an undercurrent of anger, constant power struggles, and hair-trigger reactions.

Parents need a source of wisdom, strength, and hope that's outside themselves. Paul David Tripp points us to that source:

> So your hope as a parent is not found in your power, your wisdom, your character, your experience, or your success, but in this one thing alone: the presence of your Lord. The Creator, Savior, Almighty, Sovereign King is with you. Let your heart rest. You are not in this parenting drama alone. Your potential is greater than the size of your weaknesses, because the One who is without weakness is with you, and he does his best work through those who admit that they are weak but in weakness still heed his call.[19]

Human beings are flawed, and marriage brings out those flaws more than any other relationship. Disagreements and conflicts are inevitable, but they don't have to be destructive. In fact, marital squabbles can actually become opportunities for growth. We can compare the healthy resolution of annoyances to the process of refining gold. Gold ore has a lot of impurities. In fact, a ton of ore may contain only a fraction of an ounce of gold, so the smelting process is extensive. When gold was mined hundreds of years ago, the rock was heated until the impurities separated from the gold. The process was repeated several times until pure gold was left. In the same way, the impurities of selfishness that exist in all of us can be melted by the heat of mutual frustrations. The result can be the beautiful gold of understanding, compassion, patience, and deeper, richer affection.

Recasting Your Reaction

Let me offer some time-tested steps to handle today's frustrations.

1. Be objective about your reactions.

Are they proportionate or disproportionate to the events?

Would an emotionally healthy, secure person respond that way? Why or why not?

2. Expect your fair share of frustrations.

We're fallen people who live in a fallen world. Things aren't the way God initially intended, and they aren't the way they'll be in the new heavens and new earth. For now, struggles are the lot of every human being. When our expectations are unrealistic, we're setting ourselves up for disappointment. Actor Antonio Banderas succinctly noted, "Expectation is the mother of all frustration."

High expectations can sound like:

- "She should know better."
- "He never . . ."
- "They always . . ."
- "I can't believe he'd do that."
- "Why does this always happen?"
- "I never get a break."
- "Doesn't he know . . . ?"

What are some of your recurring frustrations with your spouse (particularly about money, sex, in-laws, and children)?

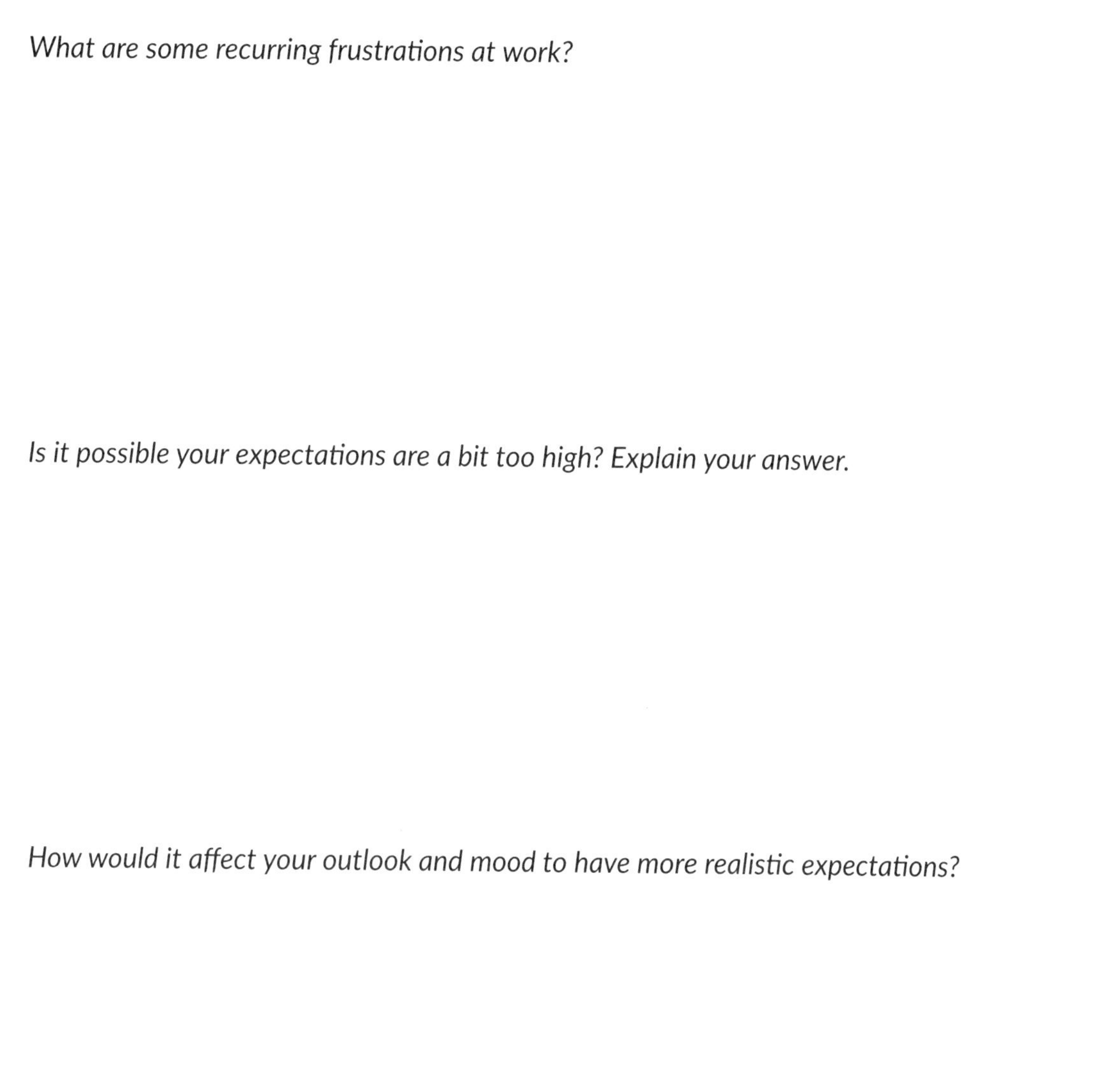

What are some recurring frustrations at work?

Is it possible your expectations are a bit too high? Explain your answer.

How would it affect your outlook and mood to have more realistic expectations?

3. Turn "I deserve" into "I can learn."

This is a game-changer. Our normal reaction to frustration is disgust, annoyance, and maybe genuine anger, but these come from the firm belief that "This isn't fair, and I deserve better!"

It's possible to reframe the frustrating event as a classroom instead of a dungeon. In a classroom (especially if it's an elective you've chosen to study), you pay attention, absorb information, and put what you learn into action. Each time someone has made you late, added to your to-do list, spilled milk, forgotten to fold the laundry, or ignored your needs, you can ask yourself, *What lesson do I need to learn in this moment? What's a good and healthy response right now?* Just asking these questions changes your point of view from entitlement to hope.

How would asking these questions help you handle your frustrations?

4. Write a better script.

What do you say (verbally or in your mind) when you're frustrated? Negative self-talk reinforces unrealistic expectations and a sense of entitlement. A friend who endured a lot of hurt in his upbringing told me that his instant reaction to even the slightest setback had been to curse (though if others were around, he cleaned it up a bit). His wife told him, "You need to find something better to say. How about, 'Oops'"? He said it had taken him a few weeks to change the habit of a lifetime, but it had made a difference. Another friend, a church leader, told me about a slogan he implemented at a conference. The weather was horrible, and many people arrived late. On the first night, everyone was terse and grumpy. Hoping to improve the sour mood, he told the participants, "Whenever we feel frustrated this weekend, say, 'You can't make it tough enough for me to complain!'" They accepted his challenge, and he said by the next morning the atmosphere had completely changed to one of positive interaction and laughter.

What's your usual script when you get frustrated? What's a better script?

5. Find an accountability partner.

My friend whose normal response had been to curse was open to replacing his old script with a new one, but he only changed because he listened to his wife. Our frustrations are often triggers to bigger reactions, so if we're serious about learning to deal with our anger, we need to enlist the help of someone who loves us enough to tell us the truth and hold us accountable. It may be a friend, a counselor, a group member, your spouse, or someone else in your family. It can be almost anyone, but it needs to be someone!

Who might be your accountability partner? How might it help to have one?

6. See frustrations from God's point of view.

God stands on the outside of time. He sees the beginning, the middle, and the end—not just of our momentary situations or even our lives, but of all of history! God used the trials of Joseph (including the betrayal by his brothers, a false charge of attempted rape, and a forgetful cellmate) to rescue his family (and all of Egypt) from starvation. And even more significantly, God used the betrayal of Jesus by all of humanity to rescue us from sin and death. God is always present, always working, and usually hiding the strings he's pulling, but he has proven to be completely trustworthy.

Many years ago, Gregory of Nyssa said that his friend Basil had "ambidextrous faith" because he took the blessings of God in one hand and life's heartaches in the other, trusting that God would use both to equip him to accomplish God's will.[20] In his book, *Reaching for the Invisible God*, Philip Yancey tells the story of a rabbi who said, "A man should carry two stones in his pocket. On one should be inscribed, 'I am but dust and ashes.' On the other, 'For my sake was the world created.' And he should use each stone as he needs it."[21] We are but dust and ashes—we don't deserve any special treatment. But the entire world was created for us—which means God has a wonderful plan to use every moment for our good and his glory.

Two passages in Isaiah give us perspective. The first is during a time of celebration, as God's people sing:

> You keep him in perfect peace
> whose mind is stayed on you,
> because he trusts in you.
> Trust in the Lord forever,
> for the Lord God is an everlasting rock. (Isaiah 26:3-4)

No matter what annoyances come up, we can have "perfect peace" if our minds are fixed on God's character, grace, strength, and promises.

Later, in the second passage, Isaiah quotes God giving assurance to his people during hard times:

> But you, Israel, my servant,
> Jacob, whom I have chosen,
> the offspring of Abraham, my friend;
> you whom I took from the ends of the earth,
> and called from its farthest corners,
> saying to you, "You are my servant,
> I have chosen you and not cast you off";
> fear not, for I am with you;
> be not dismayed, for I am your God;
> I will strengthen you, I will help you,
> I will uphold you with my righteous right hand. (Isaiah 41:8-10)

In our frustrations, we're not alone. God has chosen us, forgiven us, and adopted us as his own. Amid our immediate struggles, we can trust God for wisdom and strength . . . and he'll provide. When we see annoyances from God's point of view, we can respond with faith instead of reacting in anger.

What difference will it (or does it) make to memorize a passage of Scripture so God's perspective is always available to you?

7. Practice your response.

Use this exercise to prepare your mind and heart for frustrations to come. Like any new skill, this one takes practice. Memorize a script, identify your recurring triggers, reflect on God's perspective, and anticipate having a healthier response. If you're often frustrated by traffic delays, go through these steps. If you often are annoyed by your kids, practice these steps. Whatever the person or situation, practice will create new neural pathways in your brain, and sooner or later, a healthier response will become second nature.

Generally, what short-term advantages do you experience from your frustrations? (Yes, there are some!)

What are some disadvantages in how you express your frustrations in your relationships?

Evaluate Expectations

1. For my performance, I expect . . .

- *The factors and people who shaped this expectation are . . .*

- *Is the expectation realistic or not?*

2. My expectations for my spouse are . . .

- *Is my spouse aware of my expectations?*

- *What difference will it make to clarify my expectations?*

3. My expectations for my children are . . .

- *Are they aware of them?*

- *What difference will it make to communicate them clearly (and as often as necessary)?*

Keep a "Frustration Diary"

Buy a small notebook, and for the next two weeks, take some time every day to complete these statements:

- *Today (or yesterday, if you work on this in the morning), I was frustrated about . . .*
- *When it happened, I felt . . .*
- *The intensity of my feelings was . . .*
  [Use a scale between 0 (numb) and 10 (off the charts).]
- *My self-talk sounded like . . .*
- *My verbal reaction or response was . . .*
- *My actions were . . .*
- *My progress to apply the principles in this chapter from the last time to this time was . . .*
- *Next time, I want to respond by . . .*

Pause right now to complete these eight statements as you think about the previous 24 hours.

CHAPTER 6

FEAR AND ANXIETY: FUTURE WHAT-IFS

As we've seen, anger can be triggered by haunting memories from the past and annoyances from the present. It can also be the result of inordinate worries about the future. Insecurity makes us feel uncertain, and our minds are infinitely creative as they come up with a vast array of "what if" scenarios . . . and few of them are optimistic! What's the connection between future fears and present anger? Thanks for asking. Anger can be a reaction to perceived injustice, and worries anticipate injustice that's just around the corner.

As we consider future what-ifs, it will be helpful to examine some of the different variations of fear, including rational fear, irrational fear, phobias, worry, and anxiety.

Rational Fear

We've already pointed out that it's good, right, and normal to be afraid when you see your three-year-old teetering on the top of a slide and about to fall onto the pavement. In a flash, your amygdala kicks into gear and you set a world record in the sprint, the hurdle, and the long jump to catch her!

Our ancestors had rational fears of being eaten by tigers and bears or crushed under the feet of mastodons, but thankfully, those threats aren't on our list today. Instead, I've noticed that more people are running red lights than ever before, so when the light turns green, I always look to see if someone is speeding through the intersection. Paranoid? You decide. In 2021, crashes that involved red light running killed 1,109 people; another estimated 127,000 were injured. A months-long study monitoring safety cameras at five busy intersections in Fairfax, Virginia, found that motorists ran a red light, on average, every 20 minutes at each intersection . . . and that wasn't during peak travel times.[22] So I'd say my concerns are valid. Similarly, if you go for routine medical tests and later get a call that the doctor wants to see you immediately, rational fear of a bad diagnosis rises in your heart, and the fear isn't placated unless you hear better news than you imagined.

Rational fear is essential for functioning in a complex world. If it produces anger, the feeling is focused on someone or something that is an actual threat.

Describe the kind of anger that results from experiencing a rational fear like the ones in this section.

Irrational Fear

Past trauma puts us on edge, hypervigilant to notice *anything* that *might* harm us. The result is that we live every minute of every day with hormone levels that are only meant to be released in real emergencies, so irrational fear creates the paradox of being very alert yet very tired most of the time. Our deep hurts in the past cause us to exaggerate genuine existing threats and see others that aren't really there. It's not uncommon to shift our fear from our own safety to that of our children (or siblings or others we care about deeply). A woman who had been physically traumatized as a girl imagined her daughter was at risk for sex trafficking. The mom had seen enough horror stories on the news to become obsessed by this threat, even though her family lived in a very safe suburb. Irrational fear may or may not be focused on a specific perceived threat, but it often produces a wave of ongoing, unhealthy anger.

Describe the nature of anger that results from irrational fears.

Phobias

Many people struggle with persistent and often debilitating fears of objects or persons that don't present any actual threat. I know a very competent high school counselor who is terrified of spiders. She has a panic attack when one touches her, and even the sight of one triggers extreme revulsion. Another friend was in a car accident and hurt his neck. He lived with the pain for years until a doctor finally convinced him to have an MRI. The tech routinely asked, "Sir, do you have claustrophobia?" He almost laughed as he said "No." Yet no sooner was he positioned into that tightly confined space than he had a full-blown panic attack. He lived with his pain another five years before his doctor assured him he could be put under general anesthesia during the procedure.

These two examples may cause some people to shake their heads and say, "Oh, come on. That's no big deal." But for people who struggle with phobias, it's a *huge* deal. Their irrational fear is more real and persuasive than any well-meaning assurances (or guilt trips). In fact, people with phobias can be very angry at those who tease them about their fear.

How can phobias trigger the reaction of anger?

Concern, Worry, and Anxiety

As we've seen, *concern* about people and situations is entirely good and normal, but *worry* is "concern out of bounds." *Worry* comes from an Anglo-Saxon word that meant "to strangle"; it's a choking feeling when we experience a significant problem. Worry is primarily a mental process, but *anxiety* goes beyond the mind and can affect the physical body with headaches, digestive problems, tense and sore muscles, and in more extreme cases, heart problems.

Anxiety is a general feeling of unease usually caused by the mental gymnastics of ongoing worry about a person or a problem. If we continue to worry about a specific matter, anxiety threatens to expand the limits of our concern. For instance, worry focuses on revising the budget so you can pay the bills at the end of the month, but anxiety is an amorphous, global dread that your life is going to fall apart. Worry subsides when the problem is resolved, but anxiety finds new reasons to accelerate the sense of doom. Worry can sharpen decision-making skills; anxiety makes it harder to think, plan, and then execute the plan.

What are some ways anxiety can produce anger?

What If . . .?

Many of us live anxious lives. We've lived so long with a nagging dread of the future that we can't imagine life without it. We may read the Bible and pray, but for some reason, God's presence and power haven't yet penetrated to the deep recesses of our hearts where this anxiety thrives. We need clear perception about our fears of the future. Here are some common ones:

- "What if people knew the worst about me?"
- "What if people ignore me?"
- "What if speaking up will only make things worse?"
- "What if I'm ridiculed or mocked?"
- "What if I don't have what it takes?"
- "What if people I love just walk away?"
- "What if I'm too vulnerable?"
- "What if I never get out of debt?"
- "What if I fail in school or my job?"
- "What if people knew me? They wouldn't like me."

- "What if I die young?"
- "What if someone I love gets very sick?"
- "What if our institutions fail?"
- "What if artificial intelligence takes over?"

Your specific fears of the future may be very different from any of these, but all kinds of fear and anxiety have a direct link to flashes of anger and lingering resentment. You can't deal with your anxiety until you've identified it.

When you think about what might happen, what scenarios come to mind, and what emotions accompany those thoughts?

The Dark Side of Anger

Unrelieved fear, worry, and anxiety can eventually take us where none of us wants to go: *depression.* The causes are many and varied, and the severity falls on a broad scale. Depression may be caused by physiological problems, such as COVID-19 or the flu. It can be the result of a chronic illness or the lack of sufficient light in northern regions, but it most often results from the loss of hope and meaning. When we're depressed, we experience changes in sleep patterns (too much or too little) and eating (again, too much or too little). We have little interest in sex, we no longer experience pleasure in things we used to enjoy, and we're unable to function normally. People who are depressed look through a dark lens at everyone and everything.

Far too often, well-meaning Christians give advice like, "Just pray about it," or, "Trust God and you'll be fine." But advice like this heaps guilt and confusion on top of the already bleak outlook. Several centuries ago, Puritan pastor Richard Baxter preached a sermon on "over-much sorrow"—what we would call depression today. He identified several possible causes. Yes, spiritual issues like guilt can play a part, but so can physical, relational, and emotional difficulties. He was far ahead of his time with his more nuanced and complex view of depression.[23]

Some might wonder if depression and grief are the same thing. They may feel the same, at least for a while, but they're different. Grief is a response to a specific loss. We may associate grief with the death of someone we love, but we grieve *any* loss. Grief is focused, but depression is dispersed and pervasive. Grief takes time, but leads to acceptance and wisdom on the other side. Depression devours our time and offers little or no hope of anything good in the future . . . unless we do something about it. Anger at the loss is often an element of the grieving process, but sooner or later, the anger is spent and life goes on. In depression, resentment and self-pity don't end until the depressed person gets adequate help from counseling, and perhaps medications.

What are some differences between temporarily having a bad day and suffering from depression?

Redirecting Our Fear of the Future

It's helpful to consider a strategy that includes actions we can take before, during, and after the fear surfaces.

Before

1. **Identify your insights.**

   In this chapter, you've reviewed the similarities and differences between rational fear, irrational fear, phobias, concern, worry, and anxiety. What insights have you received so far?

2. Lean on God.

Let's look at two passages that remind us of God's love and faithfulness. First, Solomon reminds us:

Trust in the Lord with all your heart,
    and do not lean on your own understanding.
In all your ways acknowledge him,
    and he will make straight your paths.
Be not wise in your own eyes;
    fear the Lord, and turn away from evil.
It will be healing to your flesh
    and refreshment to your bones. (Proverbs 3:5-8)

God sees into the future; we can't. His purposes for us are good and right. While we live in the world, we'll experience our share of heartache and uncertainty, but God's goodness, wisdom, and love never change. We can trust him whether the road ahead is clear or whether it looks like a dead end. We've seen that worry is based on the assumption that we know more than God about how life should go. Solomon tells us, "Don't think you're so wise! It's self-destructive to trust in yourself instead of the sovereign King of the universe! When you trust in him, especially during hard and uncertain times, you'll experience "the peace that surpasses all understanding" (Philippians 4:7).

A second passage comes from Jesus' most famous sermon—the Sermon on the Mount. He called people to follow him no matter where he might lead them, and he anticipated their fear of an uncertain future. He used some examples from the natural world to reassure them of his faithfulness:

> "Therefore I tell you, do not be anxious about your life, what you will eat or what you will drink, nor about your body, what you will put on. Is not life more than food, and the body more than clothing? Look at the birds of the air: they neither sow nor reap nor gather into barns, and yet your heavenly Father

> feeds them. Are you not of more value than they? And which of you by being anxious can add a single hour to his span of life? And why are you anxious about clothing? Consider the lilies of the field, how they grow: they neither toil nor spin, yet I tell you, even Solomon in all his glory was not arrayed like one of these. But if God so clothes the grass of the field, which today is alive and tomorrow is thrown into the oven, will he not much more clothe you, O you of little faith?
>
> Therefore do not be anxious, saying, 'What shall we eat?' or 'What shall we drink?' or 'What shall we wear?' For the Gentiles seek after all these things, and your heavenly Father knows that you need them all. But seek first the kingdom of God and his righteousness, and all these things will be added to you.
>
> Therefore do not be anxious about tomorrow, for tomorrow will be anxious for itself. Sufficient for the day is its own trouble." (Matthew 6:25-34)

When we're tempted to be anxious about the future, we need to remember who we belong to. We're the children of the King, and his plans are always for our good and his glory.

3. Enlist support.

In Paul's letter to the Ephesians, he uses different metaphors to illustrate that we need each other: We're part of the family of God. We're citizens of his kingdom. We're part of God's temple, of which Christ is the cornerstone, "in whom the whole structure, being joined together, grows into a holy temple in the Lord" (2:18-22).

To walk with God in wisdom and strength, we need support from other believers—people who listen well and don't give simplistic answers to our vulnerable questions. Some of us avoid people when we feel stressed, but we need the courage to move toward someone who understands. Others rush to supportive friends to pour out their hurt, fear, and anger. That's good and fine, as long as they make sure to deal with the causes of those emotions.

4. **Filter your news feed.**

Many people today are chronically anxious because they fill their minds with dramatic accounts from the news. Each news source tries to be more extreme than the others to get more people riled up and keep them coming back. The result is that millions of listeners and viewers live in a self-imposed state of rage at those who disagree with them.

If we listen and read only those sources that agree with us, our views become increasingly extreme. Sooner or later, we're hooked. We can't get enough! It's time to turn off the television and close the social media app, or at least severely limit it. Better yet, find a source that presents both sides of the issues. You won't be as angry and anxious, and you may find common ground with some of those people you used to think were evil!

What are some specific steps you can take to:

- *Identify your insights?*

- *Lean on God?*

- *Enlist support?*

- *Filter your news feed?*

What difference will these practices make in your life?

During

1. **Be objective about the feeling.**

   For those who live with chronic anxiety, "during" is all day every day! Whether you realize your anxiety in occasional moments or it's a nagging problem, be honest about what you're feeling. Put words to your emotions (such as, "I'm afraid of . . ."), and note any physical or relational effects (such as indigestion, headache, or soreness).

2. **Be objective about the cause.**

   What's causing your fear and anxiety? Be specific. Take the time to analyze what just happened—the trigger event. It may help to bounce your perceptions off someone you trust to get clearer insight.

3. **Challenge your thoughts.**

   When stressed, we can tell ourselves things like, "I can't do this!" "I'm such a fool!" "This will never work out!" If that happens, step aside for a minute to create some psychological distance, then ask some questions like, "What's true right now?" "What's a good next step I can take?"

4. **Clarify your next step.**

   As you recall, our instinctive reaction to danger is to fight, flee, or freeze. Those feel natural and normal, but they don't take you where you need to go. By following the previous three recommendations, you'll remove yourself from the hyper-arousal stage so you can think more clearly. Every problem has a solution, and almost always, several good ones. Take time to think it through and decide on a course of action . . . and then do it!

Recall the last time you felt anxious and then go through these four steps as practice. You'll be better prepared for how to respond the next time anxiety becomes problematic.

- *Be objective about the feeling.*
- *Be objective about the cause.*
- *Challenge your thoughts.*
- *Clarify your next step.*

After

1. **Debrief.**

   It's very difficult to be reasoned and insightful if you're in the middle of an amygdala hijacking. The "before" and "during" stages are designed to calm the amygdala so your pre-frontal cortex can function properly. When it's convenient, methodically review what happened and how you reacted or responded, and then begin to incorporate the lessons you learned.

2. **Go deeper into the greatness and goodness of God.**

   The two Bible passages we examined are just the tip of the iceberg of God's character and magnificent promises. Read the Scriptures as a good student and a devoted son or daughter. Dig deep into the Gospels to understand Christ's nature, and read Paul's letters to grasp what it means to apply God's grace to our lives.

How will you benefit from a thorough debriefing after an incident of high anxiety?

Who can debrief with you?

What's your plan to go deeper in your relationship with God? (Be very specific.)

CHAPTER 7

SELF-AWARENESS AND SELF-MANAGEMENT

Bret didn't really want to come to see me, but his wife insisted. Lindsay joined him for the first session. (I'm pretty sure she didn't think Bret would be honest with me about the reason for the appointment.) To her credit, she said she was there mostly to offer her support, and she let him tell his story. "I . . . I guess I have a problem . . . I get mad, really mad," he began.

I probed a bit. "What does it look like?"

"You know, flying off the handle sometimes. Barking at the kids over little things. I'm always just one step from a blowup."

"And you're here to find some solutions?"

"That's right. My anger is hurting the people I love the most. I hope you can fix that."

I always cringe when people assume I can "fix" them, like I have a magic wand. I explained, "I'm pretty sure you can make real progress if you're committed to do the work to uncover the root causes of your anger and walk down a path to address them. Are you in for that?"

Bret nodded. I saw a tear roll down Lindsay's cheek. We talked about the process we'd follow, and I gave Bret some homework for our next time together. I asked him to draw a timeline and identify the significant events of his life he could remember—both the pleasant ones and the painful ones.

When we met the following week, Bret showed me his timeline. As he pointed out the important events, I asked him to narrate the story. He explained that his mother was an alcoholic who had a hard time keeping a job, and his father was always mad—sometimes overtly enraged at his wife,

Bret and his older sister, and anyone else who came close enough to be a target. But even when his dad wasn't an active volcano of fury, the next eruption was always expected soon.

Bret described the time his parents separated for several months because they couldn't stand each other, and he'd included the time his sister walked out the door for good when she was 19. She'd been numbing her pain with drugs, but even that wasn't enough of a relief for her to continue living in that boiling cauldron of hurt, fear, anger, and shame.

After Bret had pointed out significant events in the lives of each person in the family, I noticed a glaring omission. I asked, "What about you? Where are you on the timeline?"

His eyes widened because he hadn't thought about himself until that moment. "I was the one who tried to keep the family together."

"Tell me about that."

"I tried to help Mom be more responsible . . . make it to work on time . . . I made excuses for her hangovers. You know, all that. And I tried to protect her from Dad. Man, when he went off on her . . ."

"And your sister?"

"To be honest, I was so consumed with my parents' problems that I didn't pay much attention to her. I saw her as just another problem that caused my parents to fight. They couldn't control her, and they quit trying."

Bret spent the rest of our appointment telling me story after story about the explosions of anger between his mother and father, often followed by weeks of militant silence. It wasn't peace; it was two armies facing off on opposite sides of "No Man's Land."

When our time was up, I observed, "Bret, you haven't talked much about your own feelings during those tumultuous times. Before we meet again, think about the connection between all you've told me about your family and the anger you've come to deal with."

He looked a little puzzled, but he said, "I'll give it a shot."

When Bret walked in the following week, I could tell he had connected some important dots. I didn't even need to ask him about it. He just dove in. "I'd never seen it before," he began. "I didn't realize how much pressure I was under when I was growing up. I felt responsible for my mom's drinking and irresponsible behavior, my dad's explosions and never knowing when the next one would happen, and my sister's attempts to avoid all the chaos by taking drugs. All those years when I was trying to help them, my own anger kept building up. I didn't even realize I was angry until . . ." His voice trailed off.

"Until?"

"I didn't put it on my timeline, but before Lindsay and I got married, I was depressed for several years."

I waited for him to tell me more.

"Yeah, it was bleak. I had a new job, I lived in a different city, and it all came crashing down on me. I tried to tell myself I was just having an allergic reaction. Can you believe I could be so stupid?"

"You were just trying to make sense of things. Go on."

"I saw a doctor to try to get some help. I expected him to give me stronger antihistamines, but he looked at me and said, 'Bret, that's not your problem. You're depressed. You need help.' He gave me the name of a psychiatrist. I went to see him a few times, but then I quit. Gradually, I learned to cope better, and the depression kind of subsided."

"Kind of?"

"Yeah, it didn't feel as much like I lived in a dark fog. I functioned better. I'm sure Lindsay helped with that. She's the first person who has loved me without demanding that I fix her every problem."

"And your anger?"

"Well, that didn't go away. With having kids, something in me clicked . . . and not in a good way. When I couldn't control them, I'd get really angry. When Lindsay tried to talk to me about it, I pushed her away and blamed her." He paused for a few seconds, and then he asked, "Can you help me?"

Throughout this workbook, we've examined some practical steps to address the root causes and contributing factors surrounding unhealthy expressions of anger. In this chapter, I want to combine them into a comprehensive, easily applied strategy. We'll examine two major parts of the strategy: self-awareness and self-management.

Self-awareness

1. See it.

In every chapter, I've invited you to open your eyes to see elements of the full range of anger, from healthy to unhealthy—a *response* to injustice or a *reaction* to misplaced expectations. I've also asked you to look beneath the surface to identify unhealed wounds that might make you feel vulnerable and fragile . . . and perhaps driven by resentment and self-pity. By now, you've probably seen more connections than ever between past hurts and present anger, and as time goes on, you'll undoubtedly gain more insights into the causes of your anger.

2. Feel it.

Most people feel threatened by anger. It's uncomfortable at best and out of control at its worst, but we need to acknowledge the hurt, frustration, and fear that almost always reside under the surface. Many of us have spent years suppressing our emotions, minimizing the primary emotions hidden behind the secondary emotion of anger, and excusing the people who have hurt us because it was too threatening to be honest with them. Now, it's important to feel the anger, but it's even more valuable to identify and understand the hurt and fear.

3. Own it.

We may have spent decades intentionally or unconsciously avoiding the painful truth about the people who hurt us, our timidity in not speaking up, and the residual damage in our lives and the lives of those we love. The truth may be hard to admit, but it's essential if we're going to move forward.

4. Make the mental switch.

One of the most essential parts of a successful strategy is using unhealthy anger as a stepping stone to emotional growth and relational change. At any point when unhealthy anger rises, you have an opportunity to repent, reject destructive reactions, and choose constructive responses instead. This includes identifying and owning what's going on in you, apologizing to those you've hurt, and addressing the underlying causes. With God's help, every experience of anger can become a growth opportunity for you.

5. Embrace God's grace.

What is your mental picture of God's character? Our family backgrounds "imprint" particular concepts of God on our young hearts. If our parents have been sufficiently affectionate, attentive, and wise, we'll probably see God in a similar way. If not, we may project their faults onto God, believing he's either harsh and demanding or distant and uncaring. We may presume that God shakes his head in disgust when he thinks of us, or we may believe he doesn't think about us at all.

The Psalms provide incredibly honest descriptions of the complete range of human emotions. We find praise and thanksgiving, certainly, but we also read about discouragement, hopelessness, anguish, and despair. In the first half of Psalm 73, the writer Asaph is furious at God. He accuses God of being unfair because ungodly people are thriving and he's not, and he responds by pouring out his resentment and self-pity. Suddenly, however, God gives him a different, more accurate perspective: someday God will make all things right, justice will reign, and it will all make sense. This change of perspectives didn't just change Asaph's mind, it changed his emotions and attitudes:

> When my soul was embittered,
> when I was pricked in heart,
> I was brutish and ignorant;
> I was like a beast toward you.
> Nevertheless, I am continually with you;
> you hold my right hand.
> You guide me with your counsel,
> and afterward you will receive me to glory.
> Whom have I in heaven but you?
> And there is nothing on earth that I desire besides you.
> My flesh and my heart may fail,
> but God is the strength of my heart and my portion forever. (Psalm 73:21-26)

Have you ever been so angry that you were like a wild animal? Asaph was, but God didn't turn his back on him. When Asaph was at his worst, God reached out to hold his hand and assure him of his great love. With Asaph's new and improved understanding, he trusted God to lead him, and he ended this section of his poem by praising the God of infinite love, wisdom, and power.

Asaph experienced the undeserved but overwhelming grace of God, but nowhere is the mind-boggling love and grace of God more evident than in the willingness of Jesus, the Son of God, to sacrifice himself as an atonement for our sins. He loves us so much that he was willing to die in our place. Jesus took the punishment we deserve so we can experience God's forgiveness, love, honor, and acceptance.

Christian faith is more than a theological doctrine, as important as that is. Our belief is not in a doctrine, but in the tender, compassionate, strong love of God poured out in us through the sacrifice of Jesus and the eye-opening power of the Spirit. If our hearts aren't melted and molded by that reality, our faith is far from complete.

The more we choose to experience the security and freedom found in God's amazing grace, the more confident we become to be honest about our anger and trust God to change us from the inside out. Why is God's grace and forgiveness so important, especially to those with anger issues? Because we can forgive those who hurt us only to the extent *we* experience God's great love and forgiveness for *our* sins. We've looked at Ephesians 4 a couple of times already, but here's another section that directly addresses anger: "Let all bitterness and wrath and anger and clamor and slander be put away from you, along with all malice. Be kind to one another, tenderhearted, forgiving one another, as God in Christ forgave you" (Ephesians 4:31-32). In other words, if we're having trouble forgiving people, it means we need to go deeper into God's grace so our hearts are filled and overflowing.

And if you keep reading through Ephesians, the next two verses provide even more understanding of grace and our motivation to love and forgive others: "Therefore be imitators of God, as beloved children. And walk in love, as Christ loved us and gave himself up for us, a fragrant offering and sacrifice to God" (5:1-2). We're called to follow God's example—not under threat of punishment, but because we're "beloved children" who delight in pleasing our Father. We may have walked in resentment in the past, but now we "walk in love." How is that possible? Because Christ loved us so much. He died the death we should have died, and he lived the life we couldn't live. We aren't accepted because we're good enough—it's all about grace.

What difference does this make? Every difference! Jesus said, "Out of the abundance of the heart, the mouth speaks" (Luke 6:45). What is the abundance of your heart? If it's anger, many people try to control it by sheer determination. They may appear to succeed for a while, but they only bottle up their anger. When it comes out in one way or another—and it will—it's never pretty! True heart change is essential so we can draw from a deep reservoir of love, strength, and wisdom as we relate to people—those who love us, those who ignore us, those who have betrayed us, and even those who will hurt us again.

Write a plan to increase your self-awareness so you . . .

- *See it.*
- *Feel it.*
- *Own it.*
- *Make the mental switch.*
- *Go deeper into grace.*

Which of these will be relatively easy for you?

Which will be difficult?

What do you need to do to make real progress with them?

Self-management

1. Determine the "locus of control."

"Locus" means *place*, so this term refers to who is in control of your thoughts, feelings, and choices, especially in stressful situations. Do you retain the authority to choose your perspective and responses to difficult people, or do you give them control over your emotions and reactions? For far too long, many of us have reacted instead of responding. We have allowed others to dictate how we felt, what we thought, and how we acted. Now it's time to take control over ourselves.

2. Identify the underlying primary emotions.

Usually, people focus on their anger—whether seething, explosive, or some other variation—because it's so powerful and evident. As we've seen throughout this workbook, however, unhealthy anger is a reaction to past hurts, present frustrations, and fears of the future. Become an experienced detective who regularly sees beyond the obvious to reveal previously hidden emotional clues. If you do, you'll find new options for how to respond instead of simply reacting. You'll finally deal with your deepest heart issues instead of only those on the surface.

3. Be careful.

The amygdala doesn't wait to be switched to "high alert." Its response to threats is unconscious, reflexive, and immediate. Learn to do whatever it takes to avoid being hijacked, and if it still happens, do whatever it takes to calm down and engage your rational brain. If you need to take a walk, leave the room, phone a friend, or take some other action to regain your composure, do it. If someone makes fun of you for needing a break, that's one more injustice you can use to prompt healthy anger.

4. Speak the truth in love.

Let's be honest: Many of us have concluded that any response that rocks the boat when confronted by an intimidating person can't possibly be the loving thing to say or do, so we avoid saying *anything*. Others tend to use truth as a sledgehammer to get their way. Jesus spoke hard truths to the self-righteous, harsh, demanding, condemning religious leaders. Does that mean he didn't love them? No, he went to the cross to pay for their sins too! If you've leaned hard toward love (or your concept of love) and avoided saying things that need to be said, find the courage to speak up. But if you've leaned toward using your version of truth to bludgeon people into submission, it's time to do a lot more listening than talking. Like any new skill, speaking the truth in love takes practice, and we aren't very good at it at first. Don't be a perfectionist, don't be a coward, and don't excuse any bullying behavior.

5. *Prepare your response.*

This isn't rocket science. You probably don't have a hundred different scenarios that trigger your anger. By this point in the workbook, you've identified a few specific people and a few recurring situations that are flashpoints for you. For each one, take the time to prayerfully prepare your response the next time it happens . . . and it will!

But even the best preparation won't take away all the anxiety of speaking up and saying, "This is what I want in our relationship," "This is what I'll do to build a bridge of trust and communicate with respect," and "This is what I'll do if you aren't willing to work with me." So write a script of what you want to say, or at least write an outline to keep with you. When the moment comes, your amygdala will try to gain control, but your preparation will help you do what you need to do.

Practice your presentation with your sponsor, counselor, or trusted friend, and anticipate the other person's reaction. The first time you speak the truth in love almost certainly won't be the last. The other person has treated you the same way for many years, and they won't change until they're thoroughly convinced you mean what you say. That will take time, courage, and persistence on your part.

6. *Use "I" statements.*

When we use "you" during sensitive conversations ("You always do this!" or "You never do that!"), we're using blame to manipulate. Instead, own your thoughts, feelings, and choices by using "I" statements, such as: "I feel hurt when this happens," "I want a relationship based on trust and respect," or "I'm making a commitment to speak up when I need to, to set limits on how far I'm willing to go, and to set boundaries on what I'm willing to accept from you. I'll also enforce those boundaries. I know it's hard for you to believe me because I haven't followed through in the past, but this is a new day."

7. *Choose to forgive.*

Forgiveness is both a choice and a process. At some point, we might choose to forgive the person who hurt us, but as time goes on, we often realize the hurt is deeper than we realized, so we need to forgive another layer, and another, and another. We forgive as much as we can as soon as we can, but without minimizing, excusing, rationalizing, or denying what happened. Some people claim that if we forgive, all our hurt will suddenly vanish and we'll be left with perfect peace and joy. If that's ever the case, I haven't seen it. When we're honest about the wounds inflicted by someone, even when we choose to forgive, the pain remains until we've grieved the loss. Sooner or later, forgiveness truly sets us free, but it's a process to get there. Remember: hurt people hurt people, but loved people love people, and forgiven people find ways to forgive.

Trust wisely.

Forgiveness and trust are two separate things. Forgiveness doesn't demand that we trust the offender. In fact, we're foolish to trust anyone who hasn't proven to be trustworthy. If the person demands that you trust them, it's a big red flag, and that's yet another reason to withhold trust. Forgiveness is unilateral—we can offer it whether the person is sorry or not, or changes or not. Often, it's more for our benefit than the offender's. But trust must be earned over an extended time and is proven by consistently honorable behavior.

Write a plan to manage your anger more effectively.

- *Determine who is in control of your emotions.*
- *Be careful to avoid getting hijacked.*
- *Speak the truth in love.*
- *Prepare your response.*
- *Use "I" statements.*
- *Enter the process of forgiving.*
- *Trust wisely.*

Which of these will be relatively easy for you?

Which will be difficult? What do you need to do to make real progress with someone who has offended you?

CHAPTER 8

NOW WHAT?

Rachel and Rob came to see me because they couldn't resolve the tension between them. They'd been married for more than eleven years, and during that time, two issues had created recurring friction: money and kids. It didn't take long for them to pinpoint the problems: Rob was promiscuous with his spending and rigid in his parenting, while Rachel had learned to live on a budget before they married and was more patient and affectionate than Rob with their two sons. Specifically, Rachel couldn't understand how Rob could be so cavalier about his spending habits . . . and their growing credit card debt. She told me, "I don't know how he can spend so much money on fishing gear. The fish don't care if he has a new rod, braided line, and the latest lures!"

"I need my space," Rob growled. "Fishing relaxes me. Can't you understand that?" He paused for a few seconds to watch Rachel's usual reaction of disgust, and then he piled on: "Our kids are going to grow up to be addicts or thieves or bums. You never hold them accountable . . . for anything!"

"That's not true!" Rachel barked back. "If they become addicts or thieves or bums, it will be because they didn't feel loved by their father!"

Okay, I thought. *I get the picture.* For them, every day was a challenge to keep their unhealthy anger from blowing up . . . and they weren't always successful.

Many couples are on opposite sides of these two common issues, so this was nothing new to me. For about six weeks, we discussed the concepts in this workbook. After about the third appointment, Rachel was moved by my sharing that we can only forgive others to the extent we've experienced the forgiveness God pours out on us in Christ. During the next three weeks, she couldn't wait to tell me what she was learning—and experiencing—about the grace of God for her. Her attitude toward Rob was also changing. The crust of resentment that had built up over the years was melting away, and genuine love and forgiveness were evident. It was wonderful to see.

Yet each time Rachel told me more about how she was experiencing God's grace and transforming her view of Rob, he sat stone-faced. In our sixth time together, I decided to probe a bit: "Rob, isn't it terrific that Rachel is grasping more of God's love and forgiveness? Can you tell the difference it's making in her?"

"Yeah," he mumbled. "Good for her."

"Has any of what I've shared and what she's learning made any difference for you?"

Rob puffed up his cheeks and leaned back in his chair. Neither Rachel nor I knew what was coming. Finally, he spoke with great weight. "Forgiveness . . . I . . . uh . . . there are things I've done . . . things that I'm not sure can be forgiven."

I glanced at Rachel. She seemed to have no idea what he was talking about. "Go on," I invited him.

He turned to Rachel. "There are things I've never told you. Things I hoped you'd never know, but I think it's time to be honest with you."

Rachel and I waited for him to continue. After a pregnant silence, Rob explained, "When we met in college, I'd left my past behind. For me, it was a fresh start, and you were the best thing that ever happened to me. I didn't tell you . . . and I still don't want to . . . but when I was in high school, I ran with a pretty rough crowd. We drank, we did drugs." He paused again. "We stole some things, and we vandalized some houses, cars, and stores. We thought it was a lot of fun. But that's not all." Rob swallowed hard. "There was this other group of guys, I guess you'd call them our rivals. One night, we found one of them pumping gas. He'd said some threatening things to us before, but now he was alone. We beat the crap out of him. He had to go to the hospital. I saw him weeks later, and he was limping. I don't think he ever got over it. I felt awful. That happened during my senior year, in the spring, actually, and I couldn't wait to get away from him, from that group of guys, and from all we'd done together." Rob stopped for a few seconds, gathered himself, and then continued, "That's why all this talk about forgiveness doesn't work for me. The things I've done . . ." His voice trailed off, and he began to cry.

As difficult as this moment was for Rob, it was a turning point in his relationship with God and with Rachel and his sons. No more secrets. No more lies. No more hiding the painful truth. I was able to tell him about the thief on the cross next to Jesus. He had been a rebel and murderer, but he experienced the wonder of Jesus' forgiveness and the assurance of his love. I reminded Rob that before Paul met Jesus, he had been more like a terrorist than an apostle, yet he experienced forgiveness for all he had done and became a beacon of God's love, forgiveness, and grace for the rest of his life. Rob wept at the thought of being washed clean from even the worst of what he'd done. Rachel moved next to him and held him as he wept.

In this final chapter, I want to assure you that change and growth are possible, but they require courage and tenacity, and *it's always a choice*. Let's look at four choices that promise to lower the internal temperature so anger doesn't spoil relationships with those we love.

Choose the Process

Like learning to play the piano or becoming proficient in a new language, dealing with anger always has a learning curve. Five decades ago, Alvin Toffler said that in the future, people would need to acquire the ability to unlearn, learn, and relearn. The hardest of the three is unlearning. We've lived with assumptions we've treated as facts, and we're convinced that "facts don't lie."

In an article in *Forbes*, Dr. Margie Warrell asserts, "What got you here won't get you there," so growth requires new thinking and strategies. She also notes, "Assumptions kill possibilities."[24] Those of us who struggle with unhealthy anger may need to:

- Unlearn what we believe about healthy and unhealthy anger.
- Unlearn the assumption that we can't do anything to prevent an instant, amygdala-hijacked reaction to fight, flee, or freeze.
- Unlearn our flawed and destructive coping strategies.
- Unlearn our use of anger to dominate and control others.
- Unlearn the belief that getting a handle on anger is hopeless.
- Unlearn the idea that we're utterly alone in our struggle.

For instance, some of us have assumed that all anger is sinful, so we feel terribly guilty and ashamed when it rises in us. We need to realize that's a wrong assumption and unlearn the misguided strategy of suppressing the emotion. Others have been comfortable with their anger—too comfortable. They need to unlearn their use of anger to dominate people and unlearn the assumption that this kind of anger is the very best kind.

This workbook has taken us through the journey of challenging our assumptions (that is, unlearning misplaced ones), learning new truths and a workable strategy, and relearning some things we've known for a long time but have somehow forgotten. Let's return to a passage in Paul's letter to the Ephesians. He wrote a clear command, "Be angry," but he immediately qualified it: "and do not sin; do not let the sun go down on your anger, and give no opportunity to the devil" (Ephesians 4:26-27)." (In other words, don't let anger fester and poison your heart because only the devil wins when bitterness and self-pity dominate our lives.) We've said that anger is a surface emotion, and underneath are the drivers of hurt and fear. Notice that Paul didn't say, "Don't sin in your fear or hurt or frustration or grief." There's nothing in the world wrong with feeling those emotions, but if we fail to be honest and effective in processing them, they inevitably lead to unhealthy anger.

The learning curve always involves times of discouragement when it seems our progress is too slow, and bursts of excitement when things suddenly make sense. It's the proverbial "two steps forward and one step back." Don't be shaken if the process of changing from the inside out takes longer than you'd like. I can confidently assert that's true of every person I've ever counseled! Be patient, be courageous, and be tenacious. It'll pay off one day.

How would you describe the process of unlearning, learning, and relearning new strategies for dealing with your anger?

Choose Your Response

You're in charge. You have authority over your choices, including how you react or respond to anger. This point may seem self-evident, but many people have adopted the attitude of "learned helplessness." They see themselves as victims who have no power over their own lives. Indeed, they may even be victims of abuse or neglect, but they've internalized the experience so it now defines them.

Others use anger to wield power, and they don't want to give it up. Their new choice is to humble themselves, recognize the damage they're causing to themselves and others, and choose a better way to deal with their anger.

We can choose to *react* by fighting, fleeing, or freezing, or we can choose to *respond* in healthy ways:

- We become aware of our usual triggers and recognize them when they happen.
- We wade into tense conversations to better understand.
- We use healthy responses to conflict to go deeper into the love and forgiveness of God, enabling us to love and forgive the people who hurt us, frustrate us, or make us afraid.
- We know when to step into conflict and when to step away to regain composure and clarity.
- We use "I" statements to own our thoughts, feelings, desires, limits, and boundaries.
- We look for common ground, not attempting to escape or punish the other person.
- We aren't afraid of our anger. We invest it in, growing wiser and stronger.
- We develop new habits of choosing to remain calm, think clearly, and look for solutions.
- We have at least a person or two to walk with us as we create new and healthy habits.

You may have felt stuck in old patterns of thinking and old ways of reacting to opposition, but no longer. You have the autonomy and authority to choose how to respond to difficult people and situations—whether they're past experiences that haunt you, present frustrations, or worries about the future.

Look at the list of healthy choices. Which two or three will make the most difference for you? Explain your answer.

Choose to Rewire Your Brain

Neuroplasticity is a term that describes the brain's ability to change. It's often compared to how an electrician rewires a circuit to allow the current to flow where it needs to go. Some people have observed this trait in the human brain and declared it "miraculous." I prefer to say it's the marvelous way God has created us . . . so that even after years of being stuck in destructive patterns of thinking and reacting, we can be changed—not just on the outside, but in the synapses of our brains. Through the process of *neurogenesis*, cells in the brain heal and grow. Instead of being fixed by past events without the hope of change, new neurons and connections can be created by new experiences. Every new observation and every new experience stimulates the brain's transformation, including:

- Interacting with a trusted person and sharing things long hidden from sight.
- Reading and learning.
- Supportive, encouraging experiences.
- Being active, including exercise.
- Rest.
- Changing routines, like taking a different route to work.

Your brain's ability to change is both chicken and egg—it initiates positive changes from the experiences just listed (and many more), and it then enhances the ability to grow from them. Gradually, you can respond in increasingly healthy ways to the problems that used to be so debilitating: stress, frustrations, anxiety, disappointments, fear, and hurt. And little by little, new behaviors become more automatic. Your brain changes a little more every time you choose healthy responses to difficult situations: you can think more clearly, heal more fully, be calmer during times of tension, plan and strategize more effectively, and adapt more readily. You'll find yourself reacting less and responding more.

Lasting change takes place in the heart as we experience more of God's greatness and grace. With each revelation, we aren't as surprised by difficult situations or people, so our amygdalae aren't hijacked as often. We can process our feelings while they're happening and choose healthy responses in the moment. We aren't frantic to please people to win their approval, we don't feel the need to dominate them, and we don't feel compelled to become invisible to avoid tension. Neuroplasticity involves gradual change, but it's a remarkable change.

Does the concept of neuroplasticity give you a bit more hope that change can last? Why or why not?

Choose Faith

It's not unusual for people struggling with unresolved anger to have misconceptions about God. Some believe he is harsh and condemning; others think of him as distant and uncaring. Yet the Bible, and especially the Gospels, dispel those soul-crushing lies. Pastor B.B. Warfield studied every passage in the Gospels that mentions Jesus' emotions and concluded that one emotion is cited more than all the others combined: his *compassion*.[25]

Compassion is revealed most clearly in response to those who are hurting or in need, and a caring person reaches out in kindness instead of contempt. We see this as a full-time trait in Jesus' life. His love never fails. Time after time he reached out to touch and heal lepers (from both their disease and isolation), heal the lame, enable the deaf to hear, restore sight to the blind, and demonstrate infinite patience with those who were slow to grasp the truth about who he was. Even when he spoke hard truths to hardhearted religious leaders, he hoped to draw them into his love; he didn't despise them. He identified their needs and then responded to care for them.

Did you pick up this workbook as merely an academic exercise? Probably not. I suspect you wanted help understanding and dealing with a painful emotion that has consumed too much of your life and hurt too many people close to you. Jesus hasn't turned his back on you. He invites you to experience his grace, love, comfort, and strength. When life seems to be too much for us, we need to hear his invitation: "Come to me, all who labor and are heavy laden, and I will give you rest. Take my yoke upon you, and learn from me, for I am gentle and lowly in heart, and you will find rest for your souls. For my yoke is easy, and my burden is light" (Matthew 11:28-30).

The cross is the measure of God's love for us. Jesus paid the ultimate price of carrying the weight of all our sin on himself, and he suffered judgment so we could become God's beloved, secure children. The message of the gospel includes much more than forgiveness for our sins (as marvelous as that is); it also means the Creator and King of the universe has adopted us as his own.

Jesus told us, "I will never leave you nor forsake you" (Hebrews 13:5). In response to his gracious promise, we can tell him, "Lord, I belong to you." Years ago, a pastor recommended that we carry that insight into every circumstance we encounter:

- When God gives us wonderful encouragement, we can rejoice and say, "Lord, I belong to you, and I realize you are the one who gave me this gift. Thank you so much!"
- When we're lonely, we can pour our hearts out to God and say, "Lord, I belong to you, and I know you are with me right now."
- When we're filled with unhealthy anger, self-pity, envy, or jealousy because life doesn't seem fair, we can pray, "Lord, I belong to you, and you have the right to determine my circumstances."
- And when we face difficulties and excruciating decisions, we can tell him, "Lord, I belong to you, and I know you will lead me and use this situation to make me more dependent on you, no matter how it turns out."[26]

So, no matter what, choose faith. Cling to God when you're angry and when you're content, when life seems to be going off the rails and when things are working out exactly like you hoped. Be thoroughly and completely honest about your anger, identify its sources, and choose to respond in healthy ways to move forward courageously, holding God's hand each step of the way.

Now, at the end of this last chapter, it's time to ask, "What now?" Describe how what you've learned will make a difference—in you and in your relationships—to:

- *Choose the process.*
- *Choose your responses.*
- *Choose to rewire your brain.*
- *Choose faith.*

Endnotes

1 Frances Schaeffer, *True Spirituality* (Carol Stream, IL: Tyndale House, 1971), p. 109.

2 Though adapted by more modern poets, this poem traces back to a song recorded in 1923 by Irving Kaufman titled "I Love Me (I'm Wild about Myself)," https://archive.org/details/78_i-love-me-im-wild-about-myself_irving-kaufman-mahoney_gbia3019160a

3 "NIH-Funded Clinical Trial Links Frequent Anger to Increased Risk of Heart Disease," NIH, May 1, 2024, https://www.nih.gov/news-events/news-releases/nih-funded-clinical-trial-links-frequent-anger-increased-risk-heart-disease#:~:text=Findings%20demonstrate%20impairment%20of%20blood,the%20National%20Institutes%20of%20Health

4 John Powell, *Why Am I Afraid to Tell You Who I Am?* (Chicago: Argus, 1969), p. 25

5 Harriet Lerner, *The Dance of Anger* (New York: William Morrow Paperbacks, 1985), p. 1

6 Susan Jeffers, *Opening Our Hearts to Men* (New York: Fawcett Columbine, 1989), p. 35

7 Gary J. Oliver and H. Norman Wright, *When Anger Hits Home* (Chicago: Moody, 1992), pp. 78-79

8 Pete Walker, "Shrinking the Inner Critic in Complex PTSD," http://www.pete-walker.com/shrinkingInnerCritic.htm

9 Dr. Bessel Van Der Kolk, *The Body Keeps Score* (New York: Penguin, 2014), p. 62

10 Diane Hamilton, "Calming Your Brain During Conflict," *Harvard Business Review*, December 22, 2015

11 Stephanie Manes, "Making Sure Emotional Flooding Doesn't Capsize Your Relationship," The Gottman Institute, https://www.gottman.com/blog/making-sure-emotional-flooding-doesnt-capsize-your-relationship/

12 Daniel Goleman, *Emotional Intelligence* (New York: Bantam, 1995), p. 22

13 Susan Forward and Joan Torres, *Men Who Hate Women and the Women Who Love Them* (New York: Bantam Dell Publishing Group, 1986), p. 43

14 Beverly Engel, *Encouragements for the Emotionally Abused Woman* (New York: Random House, 1994), p. vii

15 Frederick Buechner, *Wishful Thinking* (Harper San Francisco, 1993), p. 2

16 Lewis Smedes, *Forgive and Forget* (New York: Harper & Row, 1984), pp. 79-80

17 Lewis Smedes, "Forgiveness: The Power to Change The Past," *Christianity Today*, January 7, 1983

18 Frederick Buechner, Whistling in the Dark: A Doubter's Dictionary (San Francisco: Harper & Row, 1988), 57

19 Paul David Tripp, *Parenting* (Wheaton, IL: Crossway, 2016)

20 Cited by Philip Yancey in *Reaching for the Invisible God* (Grand Rapids: Zondervan, 2000), p. 69

21 Ibid., p. 93

22 Statistics from the Insurance Institute for Highway Safety (IIHS), © 1996-2024, https://www.iihs.org/topics/red-light-running#:~:text=injuries%20each%20year.-,In%202021%2C%201%2C109%20people%20were%20killed%20in%20crashes%20that%20involved,in%20red%20light%20running%20crashes.

23 Richard Baxter, "The Cure of Melancholy and Overmuch Sorrow, by Faith and Physic," http://www.digitalpuritan.net/Digital%20Puritan%20Resources/Baxter,%20Richard/The%20Practical%20Works%20of%20Richard%20Baxter%20(vol.17)/[RB]%20The%20Cure%20of%20Melancholy%20and%20Overmuch%20Sorrow.pdf

24 Dr. Margie Warrell, "Learn, Unlearn & Relearn: What Got You Here Won't Get You There," *Forbes*, June 12, 2020, https://www.forbes.com/sites/margiewarrell/2020/06/12/learn-unlearn--relearn-what-got-you-here-wont-get-you-there/?sh=46950d8f20a6

25 B. B. Warfield, "The Emotional Life of Our Lord," www.monergism.com/thethreshold/articles/onsite/emotionallife.html

26 Adapted from a newsletter by Iris Lowder, 1998.

About the Author

Gary J. Oliver, Th.M., Ph.D. is a husband, father, grandfather, university and seminary professor, marriage and family therapist, clinical psychologist, and author.

He was first trained as a theologian, receiving his B.A. from Biola University, an M.Div. from Talbot Theological Seminary, and a Th.M. from Fuller Theological Seminary . . . and then as a clinical psychologist, receiving an M.A. and Ph.D. in psychology from the University of Nebraska in Lincoln. He is a licensed clinical psychologist in both Arkansas and Colorado as well as a Clinical Fellow and Approved Supervisor of the American Association for Marriage and Family Therapy (AAMFT). He is also the Senior Facilitator with the *Going Deeper Together* ministry and facilitates four-day emotional, relational, psychological, and spiritual growth intensives for small groups of men and women.

Dr. Oliver has authored over 350 professional and popular articles and over twenty books, including *When Anger Hits Home, Real Men Have Feelings Too,* and *It's All About Relationships: Emotional & Relational Intelligence (ERQ)* with Dr. David H. Olson.

He has over 35 years' experience in individual, premarital, and marital and family counseling, in addition to corporate consulting. He continues to teach and provide professional training both nationally and internationally, including speaking to over a million men in live venues for Promise Keepers. He was the founding Executive Director of *The Center for Healthy Relationships* and is Professor Emeriti of Psychology and Practical Theology at John Brown University.

Gary teaches, trains, and consults with church and parachurch ministries, community organizations, corporations, seminaries, and Christian colleges and universities both nationally and internationally, where he helps strengthen relationships with a special focus on marriage enrichment, leadership development, conflict management, and Emotional and Relational Intelligence (ERQ).

CERTIFIED
Mental Health Coach
FIRST RESPONDER TRAINING

LIMITED TIME SCHOLARSHIP
No cost to the church and tuition is FREE for students!
(One-time $54 tech support fee applies)

"Without question, this training will be one of the most, if not the most, significant projects we have ever done in the history of the AACC. We need an army of helpers in the local church—those of whom God has given natural gifts and talents to offer help, hope, and guidance to the hurting!"

Dr. Tim Clinton, President
American Association of Christian Counselors

Introducing the Mental Health Coach Training, a 42-hour, biblically-based training that consists of three courses. Enroll and successfully complete all three courses and become a **"Certified Mental Health Coach"** by the International Board of Christian Care.

Our 2023 mission is to engage, educate and equip an additional 6,500 churches and congregations and to train 45,000 students all over America and around the world.

Who can enroll? Under the discretion of your church, **anyone with a calling to offer help, hope, and encouragement** to those who are hurting and looking for guidance and direction in everyday life.

- 42-hour, Biblically-based, clinically-excellent training program
- Featuring some of the world's leading mental health and ministry experts
- Study anywhere, anytime, at your own pace, on any of your favorite devices!
- On-demand video lectures—No schedules!
- Available 24/7/365
- And you have one year to complete your course

Learn to help those who struggle with **Serious Mental Illness (SMI)**, including topics like:

- Addiction
- Trauma and Abuse
- Grief and Loss
- Boundaries
- Panic Disorders
- PTSD
- Phobias
- Suicide
- Crisis Intervention
- Depression
- Stress and Anxiety

and more!

LIGHTUNIVERSITY.COM/MENTALHEALTHCOACH

6-Week Introductory Study of Biblical Counseling

COFFEE CUP COUNSELING
training program

Anger, Depression, Stress, Loss, Betrayal...

A Six-Week Introductory Study of Biblical Counseling
(complete with a leader's guide)

"WHAT TO SAY WHEN YOU DON'T KNOW WHAT TO SAY; WHAT TO DO WHEN YOU DON'T KNOW WHAT TO DO."

Lessons Include:

Week 1: Caring for People in Need
- Tim Clinton, Ed.D.

Week 2: Models of Care
- Ron Hawkins, D.Min., Ed.D.

Week 3: Becoming a Great Listener
- Mercy Connors, Ph.D.

Week 4: Relying on the Scriptures and Prayer
- Ron Hawkins, D.Min., Ed.D.

Week 5: Resources and Referrals
- Mercy Connors, Ph.D.

Week 6: Getting Started
- Tim Clinton, Ed.D.

In the six weeks of training, you'll learn:

- The privilege and responsibility of stepping into people's lives when they're most vulnerable
- The biblical basis of caring friendships
- A time-tested, three-step model of helping
- How to care for people in times of crisis
- How to become a skilled and effective listener
- How to address the difficult issues of abuse and boundaries
- How to establish a network of competent professionals for referrals
- And many other insights and practical skills you can use!

1-800-526-8673 • AACC.NET

Resources

MORE WORKBOOKS IN THIS SERIES

To order these workbooks, go to www.aacc.net

THE CHRISTIAN COUNSELING WORKBOOK SERIES
A Guide to Holistic Recovery
HOPE & HEALING FOR FOOD ADDICTION
WRITTEN BY
RHONA EPSTEIN, PSY.D

THE CHRISTIAN COUNSELING WORKBOOK SERIES
A Guide to Help Overcome Life's Challenging Moments
HOPE & HEALING FOR DEPRESSION
GREGORY L. JANTZ, PH.D
WITH KEITH WALL

THE CHRISTIAN COUNSELING WORKBOOK SERIES
A Guide to Healing Through Loss
HOPE & HEALING FOR GRIEF
WRITTEN BY
KEVIN ELLERS, D. MIN.

More titles available at www.aacc.net

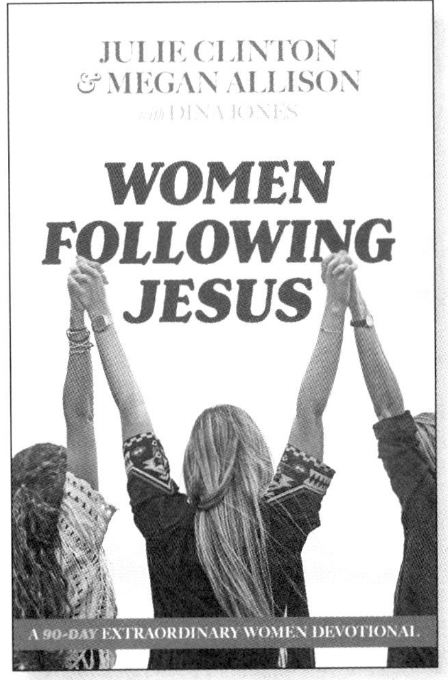